CHRISTMAS

A CELEBRATION

CHRISTMAS
A CELEBRATION

ANNETTE SPENCE
RECIPES BY CAMILLE CUSUMANO
CRAFTS BY ROBIN HANSEN

Illustrated
Books

A FRIEDMAN GROUP BOOK
BDD Illustrated Books
An imprint of BDD Promotional Book Company, Inc.
1540 Broadway
New York, N.Y. 10036

ISBN 0-7924-5840-0

CHRISTMAS: A CELEBRATION
was prepared and produced by
Michael Friedman Publishing Group, Inc.
15 West 26th Street
New York, New York 10010

Designer: Lori Thorn
Photography Editor: Ede Rothaus

Color separations by Scantrans Pte Ltd.
Printed in Hong Kong and bound in China by Leefung-Asco Printers Ltd.

Dedication

To Bubba and Allen and all our Christmases back home.

Contents

Introduction

Why are red and green the traditional colors of Christmas? What two books of the New Testament tell the story of the first Christmas? What's the recipe for eggnog? Why is mistletoe a somewhat ominous plant to be associated with the holidays? And what female actress starred in the TV remake of the movie classic, "It's a Wonderful Life"?

From the practical to the trivial, from the history to the mystery, *The Encyclopedia of Christmas* is the answer book for everything that has to do with this merry time of year. Arranged in alphabetical entries

✦ from Advent to Yule Log, the following pages can serve as a manual for craft, decorating, and party ideas, or as a coffee-table book full of intriguing facts and stories. Learn how to make your own ornaments or discover the origin of Santa Claus—the information is right here.

Compiling a complete manual on such a subject is a challenging task, but not as circumscribed as one might expect. Christmas has evolved into more than event—more, even, than a season—into an adjective that applies to a catalog of nouns all the year round. There are Christmas TV shows,

✦ Christmas plants, Christmas cards, and Christmas Seals.

This category is so broad, in fact, that many people have mourned the original purpose of the holiday—to celebrate the birth of the Christian messiah, Jesus.

Yet for all the hype and clutter, at the very core of the great, big world of Christmas—and of this book—is the story of Jesus's birth. As for Dickens, diets, and dolls, they have a place, too, even if they're somewhat removed from the purpose of this colossal celebration.

Here's wishing you a merry Christmas.

Annette Spence

· · · · · · · · ·

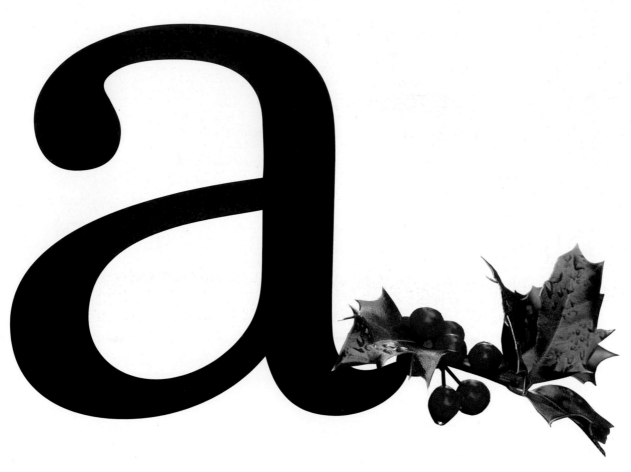

Advent

The term advent comes from the Latin word *adventus*, which means "a coming." The Advent season includes the first four Sundays before Christmas and reminds Christians of the coming of Jesus. Many Christians, particularly those in Germany and other European countries, observe Advent with fasting and prayer. The first Sunday of the season is known as Advent Sunday.

The wreaths and calendars used to celebrate this religious holiday are, in fact, German customs. For each of the four Sundays, a red candle is added to an Advent wreath made of fir, holly, or laurel. Advent calendars typically show a Christmas scene incorporating little doors or windows that are opened, one at a time, on each of the twenty-five days preceding December 25. The largest door is opened on Christmas Day

and often shows a picture of Jesus, Mary, and Joseph. Some Advent calendars consist of one big star and twenty-four little stars, designed to be removed daily until only the large star remains on Christmas Eve. There also are Advent calendar candles, numbered on one side, which are burned down one number each day from December 1 until Christmas. They are usually lit during a family meal. (*See also Wreath.*)

Advent Gift Calendars

Calendars make exceptionally useful holiday gifts. Unlike Christmas ornaments, candles, and other seasonal paraphernalia, which are given as gifts on Christmas Day, Advent gift calendars are presented at the start of the season, when they will still be useful.

An Advent gift calendar can have any sort of Christmas theme. Some have room for twenty-four presents to be tied

on. There isn't one for the 25th, when there are so many other gifts exchanged. In Europe, Advent calendars are more varied than Christmas stockings are in this country and often take forms other than the traditional calendar. The calendars can be as varied as a silk-screened cloth depicting preholiday activities in the Christmas elf kingdom, with presents hanging from twenty-four brass rings; a silk-screened cloth showing Santa sitting in his sleigh atop twenty-four pockets suitable for twenty-four miniature chocolate bars; and a children's book filled with twenty-four very short pre-Christmas stories and small activities, some crafts, and family games.

The Advent Heart Calendar shown on page 3 was appliquéd by hand in very short order and has twenty-four rings to hold presents. The hearts are scraps of red, blue, and orange felt or coating, stitched onto a larger piece of blue

woolen coating. Because the wool has been fulled during manufacturing, there are no ravelly edges that need hemming. Generally the stitches used for appliquéing are rather large, using all six strands of embroidery floss, so the work goes quickly. The calendar can, however, be made of a deep blue or dark green cloth with hearts of different red cotton prints, with the edges machine hemmed.

The Advent Picture Calendar is fun to make if you enjoy painting or drawing, but it can also be made by pasting a scene to a thin piece of cardboard and finding small motifs from wrapping paper and old Christmas cards to hide inside the windows. Very young children enjoy receiving these and thrill to the discipline of opening only one each day. Older children can be talked into making them for younger cousins. Be aware, however, that twenty-four is a large number of pictures for most children to produce, and you may have to fill in a few yourself.

ADVENT HEART CALENDAR
· · · · · · · · ·

Materials:
16- by 22-inch piece of dark blue or green coating, felt or fabric
9- by 12-inch pieces of red, orange, and dark blue felt coating or other thick fulled fabric
sewing machine
navy blue thread
bright-red cotton or wool embroidery thread
2 dowels, ½ inch by 21 inches
yarn or red string for hanging
24¾-inch brass or plastic curtain rings
red Coats & Clarks crochet cotton

1. Cut dark blue or green fabric; pin hearts in place, leaving 2½ inches at top and bottom for hem and dowel.

2. Cut small hearts from 9- by 12-inch fabrics. Red and orange hearts are invisible-stitched in place, but without turning under if using heavy wool fabric or felt. Blue hearts are blanket stitched with red wool. The more pins you use, the better, as you don't want the hearts or the background to slip.

3. Hem the edges of the calendar with a machine, turning only 1¼ inch under. Do not turn under twice, as this fabric doesn't fray.

4. If using brass rings, stitch them in place at the top of each heart. The example uses plastic rings, which were covered with single crochet with red crochet cotton.

5. Slide dowels in place in both hems and hang up with several thicknesses of red yarn or crochet cotton.

6. Tie a small gift to each of the rings.

Hanne Hansen

ADVENT PICTURE
CALENDAR

Materials:
paint, crayons
small paint brush
construction paper
glue (optional)
tracing paper
carbon paper
white drawing paper
sharp knife
scissors

✦ 1. Paint, draw, or paste up a wintry
picture on construction paper or
thin cardboard.
2. With a light pencil, mark the
outlines of twenty-four windows,
making the last one larger, for
Christmas Eve.
3. Transfer these outlines to a piece of
tracing paper. Then use carbon
paper to transfer them to a piece of
white drawing paper. Number the
windows outside the lines. Mark top
and bottom, left and right.

✦ 4. Draw cheery Christmas pictures in
the boxes on the white drawing
paper: teddy bears, birds, candles,
and anything that comes to mind.
You can also paste in pictures from
old Christmas cards.
5. With a sharp knife, carefully cut three
sides of each window on the big cardboard or construction paper winter
scene so that each can be opened like
a door. Glue the decorated white
paper behind the winter scene, so the
doors line up with the pictures.

Art, Christmas

If paintings and sculptures of the Virgin Mary and the infant Jesus can be considered art with a Christmas theme, then this subject is well represented. The Madonna and child rank among the most important art subjects the Christian religion has inspired. This theme is particularly prevalent in the art of the Italian Renaissance: The painter Raphael created two of the most famous pictures of Mary, *The Sistine Madonna* and *The Madonna of the Chair*; Leonardo da Vinci's painting *Virgin of the Rocks* and Michelangelo's sculpture *Medici Madonna* are other well-known works of art.

The nativity scene has inspired the work of masters as well. *The Adoration of Shepherds* by Giorgione, a Venetian who lived until 1511; *The Nativity* and *The Adoration of the Magi*, by Sandro Botticelli, an Italian Renaissance painter; and *Holy Night* by Correggio, an Italian Baroque painter who, like Botticelli, lived in the late 1400s and early 1500s, are all famous paintings. The work of Fra Angelico, an Italian Renaissance painter who died in 1455, is also religious in nature and includes *The Nativity* and *The Madonna of Humility*. The adoration of the babe by the three wise men has long been another popular theme in artwork. It was explored by Albrect Dürer, the German painter and engraver who died in 1528; Paolo Veronese, the mannerist Italian painter who died in 1588; and Peter Rubens, the seventeenth-century Flemish master.

In the last two hundred or so years, American painters, illustrators, and printmakers have also captured a wealth of holiday images. The materials range from simple wood carvings and hand-drawn cards to sophisticated renderings in oil on canvas and complex printing processes. Many of our best-loved Christmas images, such as Winslow Homer's 1865 wood engraving *Christmas-Gathering Evergreens* and H. Schile's 1870 colored lithograph *Christmas Tree*, date from the nineteenth century, when both life and art were simpler.

But even during the Victorian age, Christmas wasn't always depicted in a gay fashion; the site of Eastman John's 1864 oil-on-canvas *Christmas Time: The Blodgett Family* is a dark, restrained Victorian parlor. More recently, painters Grandma Moses (*Out for Christmas Trees*, *Christmas at Home*, both 1946) and Norman Rockwell (*Stockbridge Mainstreet at Christmas*, 1967; *The Saturday Evening Post* cover, December 23, 1944) have contributed some of America's most memorable holiday scenes. (*See also Nativity Scenes; Wise Men.*)

"Bah, Humbug!"

Early in Charles Dickens' story *A Christmas Carol*, Ebenezer Scrooge is visited by his nephew, Fred, who bids him a

Merry Christmas. "'Bah!' said Scrooge, 'Humbug!'" And the rest is history. Because ever since Dickens published his classic in 1843, Scrooge's ill-willed oath has been the most oft-repeated line from the story, even appearing on commercial T-shirts and coffee mugs. Usually, though, "Bah, humbug!" is used in jest, since Scrooge's transformation from crabby old miser to sentimental do-gooder is widely appreciated by audiences around the world. *(See also Dickens, Charles; Poems and Stories.)*

In Charles Dickens' classic, A Christmas Carol, Ebenezer Scrooge is visited by three ghosts. The mission of the third ghost is to show Scrooge scenes from his dismal future.

Bells

Although they are not exclusively symbolic of Christmas, bells have always been closely associated with religious services. For example, Jewish high priests wore gold bells on the borders of their robes, and Emperor Augustus of Rome had a bell hung before the Temple of Jupiter. It is believed that Christians first used bells on churches about the year A.D. 400, but by medieval days, the ringing of bells had become closely associated with Christmas. Befana, the Italian gift bringer, supposedly rang her bell as she went down chimneys. St. Nicholas carried a handbell on his visits, too, and in Clement C. Moore's poem, "A Visit from St. Nicholas," Santa Claus's sleigh had bells.

Bells have inspired songs ("Silver Bells" and "I Heard the Bells on Christmas Day"), poems ("The Christmas bells from hill to hill/Answer each other in the mist"), and legends (according to religious lore, when Christ was born the devil died and for an hour before midnight the church bells were rung). In the United States street decorations feature bells, and the Salvation Army posts a bell-ringer at every charity pot. Bells turn up on wreaths, trees, packages, and other decorations, and they've been known to inspire the shape of Christmas cookies as well.

Decorating with Bells

- Wire together a string of jingle bells to make a wreath-shaped napkin ring; let your guests take them home as party favors.
- In a crystal bowl, put loose, golden jingle bells or bell-shaped ornaments (a variety of bells is just as pretty as one type); add a snippet of greens and a red ribbon to complete your centerpiece. (*See also Decorating; Music, Christmas; Poems and Stories.*)

Bethlehem (*See The First Christmas. See also Places, Christmas.*)

Birthdays, Christmas

To share the birthday of Jesus—or even to be born within a few days of December 25—is sometimes considered a misfortune. Preparations and festivities for the holidays are so demanding, the Christmas birthday is easily slighted or even forgotten. Still, the Christmas baby is in the good company of the following notables who were also born on December 25:

1642: Sir Isaac Newton, English mathematician and physicist.
1821: Clara Barton, founder of the American Red Cross.
1887: Conrad Hilton, American hotel magnate.

1899: Humphrey Bogart, American film actor.
1907: Cab Calloway, American bandleader and singer.
1918: Anwar-el Sadat, Egyptian politician and winner of the 1978 Nobel Peace Prize.
1945: Alice Cooper, pop music singer.

Boxing Day

In Great Britain and Canada, Boxing Day is usually celebrated on the 26th of December. The holiday may have originated in the custom of giving Christmas boxes to policemen, lamplighters, and servants. On that day, the alms boxes that had been placed in churches over the festive period were opened and their contents distributed. Today it is customary to recognize the work of postal workers and newspaper deliverers with bonuses.

Also known as St. Stephen's Day, Boxing Day celebrates two saints of that name. One was the first Christian martyr, who was stoned to death for blasphemy soon after Jesus' death. The other was a ninth-century missionary in Sweden. Since St. Stephen is the patron saint of horses, these animals were traditionally fed bread, salt, or corn and blessed in church by an English priest on that day. (*See also International Christmases.*)

C

Cactus, Christmas

Known botanically as the *Schlumbergera bridgesii*, the Christmas cactus got its common name from the holiday during which it blooms. Arching, drooping stems consist of bright green, flattened joints that are smooth and scallopedged. The plant gets buds around Thanksgiving. Rosy, purplish-red flowers, tubular and many petaled, appear around Christmas.

✦ Like all cacti, the Christmas cactus is not difficult to grow and only has a few simple requirements. Pot it in a light, humusy soil or African violet soil mix. Since strong light is essential for the growth and flowering of this South American succulent, keep your cactus in the sunniest window in the house. Water it more frequently during spring and summer. This is also the time to apply fertilizer. Ask your local nursery to recommend a brand.

During autumn and winter, water only enough to prevent the soil from drying out completely. This is the plant's dormant period. During the winter it's also important to water early in the morning so any surplus moisture will evaporate by nightfall. Also, during the cold season place it in an unheated room (about 45 degrees F).

✦ *The Christmas cactus is named after the season in which it blooms. The cactus may grow up to three feet across in the wild but rarely achieves that size indoors.* ✦

ETERNAL
CHRISTMAS CACTUS
MOBILE

· · · · · · · · · ·

If you don't have a green thumb, you may want to make this felt Christmas cactus, which hangs very prettily as a mobile or in a doorway as a kissing ball. It's simple to make and, unlike its living counterpart, requires no soil or attention at all.

✦ Materials:

tracing paper

1 square foot orange felt

1 square foot red felt

2 square feet green felt in light and dark shades

1-inch-diameter bead with large hole

⅜-inch-diameter bead

12-inch-long red or green pipecleaner

⅛ to ¼ inch red ribbon

✦ scissors, needle, green thread

✦ 1. Using tracing paper, trace these patterns for leaves and flowers, or cut them freehand.

2. Cut small flowers of orange felt. Cut two large red flowers for each orange one. Cut many leaves in both colors of green.

3. Using the leaves, sew chains, alternating between light and dark colors. Thread can either be anchored for each attachment or carried

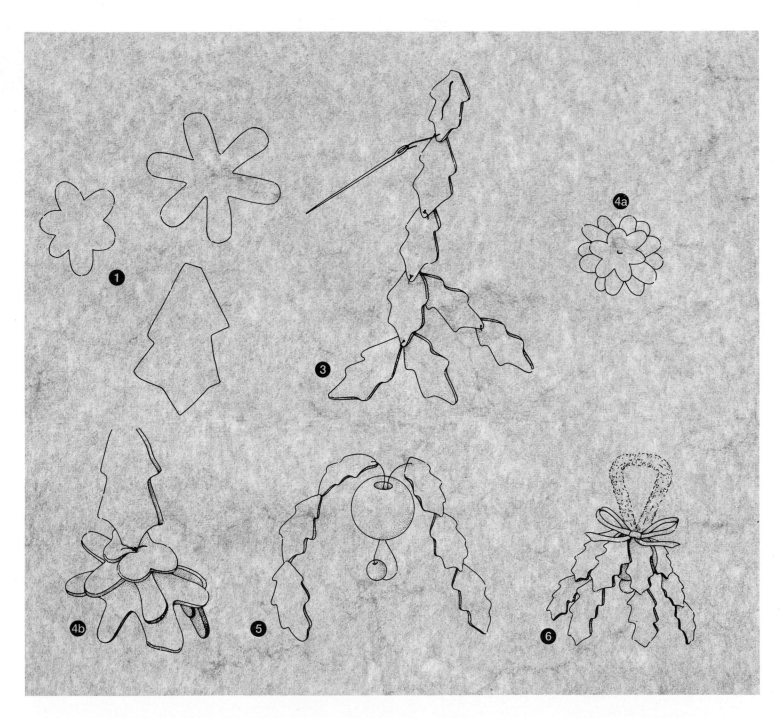

down the center of each leaf. Follow the illustration, sewing three or more leaves together in one chain and attaching "branching" sections of one or more leaves. Make five leaf chains.

4. To create flowers, layer two red flowers on top of one orange. Sew together. Then sew flowers to tips of leaves, one or more flowers per branch end.

5. Secure a thread to the leaf end of one branch and pull the stem end partially down into the large wooden bead. Draw the thread through the small bead then carry it back up through the large bead to catch a new branch end. Pull up firmly. Keep going down through both beads and coming up to catch

new branches until there are no branches left. Anchor thread firmly in a leaf and cut thread.

6. Push a long red or green pipecleaner through the large bead, through the small bead, and bring it back up through the large bead. Tighten, then twist the ends together to form a large loop. Tie a red bow at the bottom of the loop as shown.

Candles

Religious ceremonies and holidays of all types include candles, but they are especially popular at Christmas. Yuletide candles symbolize the birth of Christ, "the light of the world," and they are an important part of holiday decorations and traditions.

In the United States and Canada for example, many churches hold candlelight services on Christmas Eve. In Spain families place a burning candle above the door, whereas in Italy candles stand at the windows to light the way for the Holy Child. In England a great candle once took the place of, or supplemented, the Yule log. It was believed that the candle had to burn throughout Christmas Day or bad luck would plague the family in the coming year.

Yule candles are very popular in Scandinavia, and various superstitions used to be attached to them. In one region of Denmark two great candles stood for husband and wife, and whichever burnt down first indicated which of the two would die first. Various practices were also connected with the candle stubs. They might be used to brand a cross on the farm animals, to smear on the plough in winter, or even to feed to the hens. Lighting candles on the graves of ancestors is a fairly recent Scandinavian custom that may derive from the Viking belief that the dead return to haunt the living at the winter solstice.

Before the advent of electric lights, candles were used to decorate Christmas trees. Martin Luther, the leader of the Protestant Reformation in sixteenth-

Candles make a setting intimate and memorable. Traditionally, unused candles have been considered a sign of inhospitality. You should always light new candles — even for just a moment — before guests arrive, so the wicks will be charred.

century Germany, may have been the first to put lighted tapers on his tree, and for the next few centuries others followed his example. Because wax was expensive, most people used various forms of long, thin tallow lights, which could be wrapped around the branches. Others lighted their trees with a wick floating in oil held in half a nutshell, which was balanced in the tree. In time, these lights were replaced by heavier, more ornate candles accompanied by candleholders. The danger of fire was always inherent, and that was one reason that candlelit trees were replaced by

electrical lights by the 1920s. Because real candles are impractical, today electric fabrications decorate trees and windows all over the United States.

Decorating With Candles

- Traditional choices for Christmas candles are tall, tapered, and red; short, squat, and bayberry-scented; shaped like a Santa Claus or a bell; or simply white and scattered in assorted candlesticks.
- Cluster candles on a silver tray. This creates a sumptuous effect.
- Placing candles on mantels—where they might reflect into ornamental mirrors—sets an old-fashioned scene.
- By bringing the glow of candlelight to an area of your home, you will create a special spot. Old family photos in decorative frames look especially lovely in candlelight.
- Another idea is to wrap the glass holders of votive candles with linen and hold them in place with raffia. You might also fill a pretty bowl to the brim with white salt, then set in as many small pillar candles as you like; the salt catches drips and the effect is pretty.
- If you're very ambitious, create a centerpiece by filling a hollowed-out length of birch bark with evergreens, cones, and fruit, then adding a couple of thick candles, wedging them securely in place.
- Another striking centerpiece: Fill a large wooden cutting bowl with shiny apples, oranges, lemons, greens, and a couple of hollow grapefruits with votive candles.

(See also Decorating; Lights, Christmas; Tree, Christmas; Scents.)

DEER CANDLEHOLDER

Candles are part of the magic of the Christmas season, a warm little flame on the supper table or on the mantelpiece. Children adore the mess of making candles, but their parents don't enjoy that aspect.

This candleholder is a fun compromise. With a small amount of plaster of Paris, some tiny purchased figures, two paper cups, and some felt scraps, children can create something permanent, pretty, and nonflammable, that speaks of Christmas, will hold a real candle, and is a lot less mess to make.

However, there *is* enough mess to be interesting, so an adult should keep an eye on what's going on and for younger children, be in charge of the actual plaster pouring.

✦ Materials:
3 small plastic deer (about 1 inch tall; available in Christmas supply stores)
2 paper cups
small amount plaster of Paris
scraps of red and green felt
red or green embroidery floss
needle
scissors
standard-size candle

Making the mold:
1. Cut the bottom off one paper cup, making it 1½ inches high.
2. In the center of the cup bottom, trace a circle the diameter of the candle you will use. Cut it out carefully.
3. Cut a 1⅝-inch-high strip from the leftover top of the paper cup. Don't include the rolled top edge of the cup in this strip. Roll the strip into a cylinder, tape it together, and place it in the hole. The mold is complete.

✦ Casting the candleholder:
1. Mix small amount of plaster of Paris according to instructions on the package.
2. Pour into outer circle of mold.
3. Cut tiny scraps of red and green felt and let them fall on the surface of the plaster, to look like fallen leaves.
4. While the plaster is still soft, stand the deer in the plaster.
5. Let the plaster dry for two hours, then peel the paper cup off the candleholder.
6. Insert candle into the hole and light it.

✦ Cards, Christmas

Each year people exchange more than two billion Christmas cards with friends, family members, and business acquaintances. Yet this annual tradition of conveying good cheer via a printed greeting and connecting with acquaintances old, new, distant, or nearby is a relatively young one. Since the latter half of the 1800s, the number of greeting-card companies producing Christmas cards has expanded from a single firm to about 850 publishers.

History

The widespread sending of cards is recent, but the exchange of written greetings at the start of the new year is an age-old custom. It was practiced by the ancient Egyptians and later by the Romans. Medieval European artists made new year's good-luck greetings by engraving Nativity scenes combined with biblical phrases on wood blocks. By the eighteenth century it was customary in England to hand-deliver written new year's messages.

The Christmas card was also foreshadowed by "Christmas pieces," school compositions ornamented with pen flourishes that created borders, scrolls, and headings, as well as pictures of birds, animals, and flowers in the nineteenth-century style. Christmas pieces were created by young schoolboys as a display of penmanship for their parents.

In 1843, an English businessman named Henry Cole commissioned what may have been the first Christmas card resembling those of today. Cole asked an artist friend, John Calcott Horsley of the Royal Academy, to design a Yule greeting to send to his friends instead of the usual seasonal letters. Cole then had about one thousand copies of the three-by-five postcard printed as lithographs and water-colored by hand.

A few others had the idea of creating and sending Christmas cards during the nineteenth century in England, but it was a German emigrant, Louis Prang, who fostered the American custom. Around 1875, after opening a small lithography business in Boston and perfecting the process of making colored pictures, Prang experimented with simple flower designs and the words "Merry Christmas" on cards. By 1881 Prang was turning out more than five million cards annually.

Two of today's largest Christmas-card producers first arrived on the scene in the early 1900s. The Gibson Art Company built a huge business in the previous century distributing Prang cards, but by 1908 the company was producing its own designs. About 1910 Joyce C. Hall and his two brothers opened a specialty store near Kansas City, where they sold cards, gifts, and stationery. When they purchased an engraving firm and began making their own products, Hallmark Cards was born. Now the largest producer of greeting cards in the world, every year Hallmark offers 2,500 Christmas-card designs to choose from.

Styles
Horsley's three-paneled creation depicted poor people being fed and clothed as well as a jubilant family drinking wine together. But despite his good intentions, Cole was criticized for promoting drunkenness.

Prang's early cards were small, usually measuring two and a half by four inches, printed on one side only. They depicted subjects such as flowers, seashells, butterflies, and insects. By the end of the 1870s, the cards were larger, sometimes as much as seven to ten inches high, and the pictures, mottoes, and verses began to represent more distinctive Christmas themes. A typical example, first published in 1878, portrayed a little girl in a hoop skirt standing under mistletoe while a boy in a sailor suit tried to steal a kiss. At that time, one side of the card was devoted to the design itself; the other side was likely to carry a message longer and more creative than the previously used "Merry Christmas," as well as a short biography of the artist.

Season's Greetings

Marie Knouff

Christmas cards make a statement about the giver. Whoever selected the card above favored an old-fashioned Christmas with falling snow on the outside and a crackling fire on the inside.

As Prang's elegant cards, drawn by well-known artists and talented winners of the company's self-sponsored contests, became more popular, other types of Christmas cards flooded the market. Especially prominent were the Victorian-style creations in paper or satin and decorated with silk fringe, lace edges, embossed centers, and tassels. Some folded out like maps; others fit together like puzzles. Another favorite was the "pop-up": When opened, it revealed a tiny manger or tableau, such as children skating or making a snowman. In contrast to these beautifully designed greetings, some cheap, inartistic cards, often from foreign firms, were also introduced during this time.

The cards of the twentieth century, however, ushered in a revival of workmanship, not to mention more reasonable prices. As the postal system was further developed and printing processes improved, more cards were produced and more people were able to afford them. And though most of the old themes were still popular, each year they were presented in different ways. For example, World War I marked the end of the imported German postcards that had been popular since the 1890s and the start of enveloped cards picturing soldiers. Cards of the 1920s reflected the careless spirit of the times, with stylish flappers and Santas driving roadsters. In the thirties, cards made light of the Depression, whereas the forties marked a return to the war theme. For example, Santa carried the American flag in some designs.

Since then, cards have continued to reflect their era. In the fifties, Santas appeared in spaceships; messages of peace conveyed in the symbolism of doves were common in the seventies. Materials have also evolved, from the elaborate fringes and tassels and painstaking lithographs of the previous century to parchment, transparent plastics, thin sheets of silver or copper-colored metal, or simpler papers. Now Christmas cards are likely to be printed on recycled paper and feature animals, cartoon characters, and nostalgic scenes. As strong as ever are the traditional symbols of Christmas: the Madonna and Child, the decorated tree, poinsettias, and the jolly face and figure of Santa Claus.

Sending and Receiving Cards

- Save money by sending Christmas postcards instead of cards with envelopes—this reduces the cost of stationery and postage.
- Instead of having a professional portrait made for your cards, use a favorite snapshot from the preceding year.
- Send cards only to out-of-town friends and relatives.
- Design and print your own cards or letters; get envelopes from a stationer rather than department stores.
- Cards can be purchased at half-price about a week before Christmas.
- Even less expensive are cards bought after Christmas; save them for next year.
- Recycle old cards and entertain the kids, too. Let the children cut out the frontispiece, remount it on heavy stationery or construction paper, and write their own message inside.
- Save time by letting the whole family help you address cards—Thanksgiving weekend is a good time.
- Having a printer typeset your envelopes and family greetings is one way

to ensure neater cards and save time. However, recipients sometimes feel slighted without your personalized greeting. An alternative might be to work on cards between Christmas and New Year's, when you may have more time. The cards will be late, but they'll have more meaning.

- Do a lot of good by purchasing cards through charities.
- Also be on the lookout for more and more companies offering recycled-paper cards.
- Display cards that you receive the traditional way, by standing them on the mantelpiece, windowsill, or table, or taping them on to doorpanels.
- Clip your cards to a cord or ribbon that is draped across a wall, over a doorway, down a doorjamb, or fastened to curtain rods.
- Keep cards in a tray or basket on the coffeetable to be enjoyed by guests.

Carols, Christmas

The word carol comes from a French round dance called a *carole*. It was also the name of an English pagan song-dance performed to celebrate the winter solstice. The Christmas song of joy or praise is believed to have evolved from the mystery plays staged in or outside medieval churches. Since few people could read the scriptures, these plays dramatized stories from the Bible as a way of teaching the congregation. The actors composed songs to accompany their performances, too, and though they were not exclusively about Christmas, many of these "carols" were devoted to the Nativity. Not surprisingly, the words carol and Christmas became closely linked.

Probably the most popular carol in the world today is "Silent Night." Ironically, the hymn was hurriedly composed on Christmas Eve 1818 in

the Austrian village of Oberndorf. When Father Jose Mohr, the parish priest, discovered that the church organ was in disrepair, he quickly composed the words of a Christmas song and asked organist Franz Gruber to set them to music. "Silent Night" was completed in time for Midnight Mass and was performed by the church choir with a guitar accompaniment. Within thirty years the hymn had achieved worldwide popularity.

"O Come All Ye Faithful," a Roman Catholic hymn, is also among the best known of carols. The first known manuscript of the hymn was signed by John Francis Wade (1711–1786), a music copyist, and many scholars credit the music to him. The current, almost universal, English version has evolved over the years from several translations from the original Latin.

"O Little Town of Bethlehem," "It Came Upon the Midnight Clear," and "We Three Kings of Orient Are" may be the best-loved carols written by Americans. The words of "O Little Town…" were written by an Episcopal rector, Phillips Brooks, who was inspired by a trip to Bethlehem on Christmas Eve 1865. Three years later the music was written by Brooks' organist, Philadelphian Lewis Redner, who said he awoke on Christmas Eve with the melody in his mind.

Edmund Hamilton Sears, a Unitarian minister, wrote the words to "It Came Upon a Midnight Clear" in 1849 in Wayland, Massachusetts. The tune we now associate with it was written a year later by New York organist Richard Storrs Willis, but it was some time later that the two were put together.

"We Three Kings…" is one of the few modern carols with words and music written by the same person. The

✦ *Joseph Mohr, the pastor of*
a church in Bavaria, wrote
the words to Silent Night on
Christmas Eve 1818. The
church organist, Franz Gerber,
composed the music to the
✦ *hymn on the same evening.* ✦

Reverend John Henry Hopkins, Jr., of Williamsport, Pennsylvania, wrote it in about 1857.

Some other popular carols at a glance:

- "Angels We Have Heard on High" is a French carol believed to date from the eighteenth century.
- The words to "Away in a Manger" were written by Martin Luther for his children. The composer is unknown.
- "Deck the Halls" is a traditional Welsh tune marking the New Year.
- "God Rest Ye Merry Gentlemen" appeared in a collection of traditional English ballads in about 1770.

- "Go Tell It on the Mountain" was born of African American spirituals.
- "Hark! The Herald Angels Sing" was a result of the efforts of Methodism founder Charles Wesley (who wrote the words) and German composer Felix Mendelssohn (who composed the music). The joining of the verse and the choral work did not occur until years after both men were dead.
- "Jingle Bells" is not considered to be a true Christmas carol. Yet this simple piece of poetry set to music—composed by Unitarian reverend John Pierpont in Boston in 1856—is often included in the roster of Christmas tunes.
- The lyrics to "Joy to the World" were

written by English clergyman Isaac Watts (1674–1748), but the composer of the melody is unknown.
- "O Holy Night" is credited to Frenchman Adolphe Charles Adam (1803–1856), who is best remembered for the ballet *Giselle*.
- "O Tannenbaum" is a favorite German carol about the Christmas tree.
- "The First Noel" is an English carol believed to date from the seventeenth century.
- "The Twelve Days of Christmas" is often included among favorite Christmas carols, even though it is actually an old English song celebrating the winter solstice and the New Year. (*See also Caroling, Christmas; Music, Christmas.*)

Caroling

The custom of singing Christmas carols on the streets was born of the mystery plays of the medieval churches. In order to teach the scriptures to the congregations, actors dramatized and sang about Bible stories, many of which had a Nativity theme. After a religious service, the carolers would stroll down the street, still singing. From the churches, the words and tunes were carried to homes in Britain, Germany, France, and Hungary, where they were sung and celebrated from the fifteenth century until the early seventeenth century.

Yet in the sixteenth and seventeenth centuries the Reformation and the Puritans frowned on such merriment. So strong was the church's influence that carols almost disappeared from England in the following two hundred years.

Caroling gradually reemerged in the 1800s when collections of old carols were published in both England and America. In England, wassailers carried the wassail bowl of steaming ale from house to house and sang seasonal songs in hopes that their neighbors would replenish the contents. In North America Christmas carols began to be heard in Sunday school rooms. In France, Germany, and Hungary the experience was roughly the same. At the same time, the renewed interest led to new carols being composed and old ones being rediscovered.

Since then carols have become increasingly popular, and carol services and concerts are well attended. Traditional door-to-door caroling is not a very common practice, although groups collecting for charity are not unheard of. For those certain communities that are particularly interested in maintaining Christmas customs, the tradition of caroling will always be strong. (*See also Music, Christmas.*)

AWAY IN A MANGER

. . . .

Away in a manger, no crib for a bed,

The little Lord Jesus laid down His sweet head.

The stars in the bright sky looked down where He lay,

The Little Lord Jesus asleep on the hay.

The cattle are lowing, the Baby awakes,

But little Lord Jesus no crying He makes.

I love Thee, Lord Jesus, look down from the sky,

And stay by my side until morning is nigh.

Be near me, Lord Jesus, I ask Thee to stay

Close by me for ever, and love me, I pray.

Bless all the dear children in Thy tender care,

And fit us for heaven, to live with Thee there.

We Wish You a Merry Christmas

Traditional British

We wish you a Merry Christmas, We wish you a Merry Christmas, We wish you a Merry Christmas And a happy New Year!

Refrain: Glad tidings we bring To you and your kin; Glad tidings

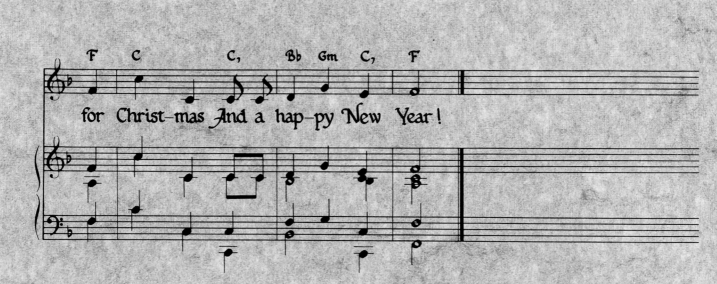

for Christ-mas And a hap-py New Year!

2. Please bring us some figgy pudding
   Please bring us some figgy pudding,
   Please bring us some figgy pudding,
   Please bring it right here!   *Refrain:*

3. We won't go until we get some,
   We won't go until we get some,
   We won't go until we get some,
   Please bring it right here!   *Refrain:*

4. We wish you a merry Christmas,
   We wish you a merry Christmas,
   We wish you a merry Christmas
   And a happy New Year!   *Refrain:*

Good King Wenceslas

Words: John Mason Neale, 1853

Music: first printed 1582

When a poor man came in sight, Gath-'ring win-ter fu——el.

2. "Hither, page, and stand by me,
    If thou know'st it, telling:
    Yonder peasant, who is he?
    Where and what his dwelling?"
    "Sire, he lives a good league hence,
    Underneath the mountain,
    Right against the forest fence,
    By Saint Agnes' fountain."

3. "Bring me flesh and bring me wine,
    Bring me pine-logs hither:
    Thou and I shall see him dine,
    When we bear them thither."
    Page and monarch, forth they went,
    Forth they went together;
    Through the rude wind's wild lament
    And the bitter weather.

4. "Sire, the night is darker now,
    And the wind blows stronger;
    Fails my heart, I know not how;
    I can go no longer."
    "Mark my footsteps, good my page;
    Tread thou in them boldly:
    Thou shalt find the winter's rage
    Freeze thy blood less coldly."

5. In his master's step he trod,
    Where the snow lay dinted;
    Heat was in the very sod
    Which the Saint had printed.
    Therefore, Christian men, be sure,
    Wealth or rank possessing;
    Ye, who now will bless the poor,
    Shall yourselves find blessing.

Silent Night

Words: Joseph Mohr, 1818; English translation anonymous

Music: Franz Xavier Gruber, 1818

Si—lent night, ho——ly night! All is calm, all is bright 'Round yon Vir—gin Moth—er and Child. Ho——ly In—fant, so ten—der and

mild, Sleep in heav—en—ly peace!

Sleep in heav—en—ly peace!

2. Silent night, holy night!
   Shepherds quake at the sight.
   Glories stream from heaven afar,
   Heav'nly hosts sing "Alleluia!"
   Christ the Saviour is born!
   Christ the Saviour is born!

3. Silent night, holy night!
   Wondrous star, lend thy light!
   With the angels let us sing
   Alleluia to our King!
   Christ the Saviour is here,
   Jesus the Saviour is here!

4. Silent night, holy night!
   Son of God, love's pure light,
   Radiant beams from Thy holy face,
   With the dawn of redeeming grace,
   Jesus, Lord, at Thy birth,
   Jesus, Lord, at Thy birth!

O Little Town of Bethlehem

Words: Phillips Brooks, 19th century

Music: Lewis H. Redner, 19th century

O lit-tle town of Beth-le-hem, How still we see thee lie!

A—bove thy deep and dream-less sleep The si-lent stars go

by; Yet in thy dark streets shin—eth The ev-er-last-ing

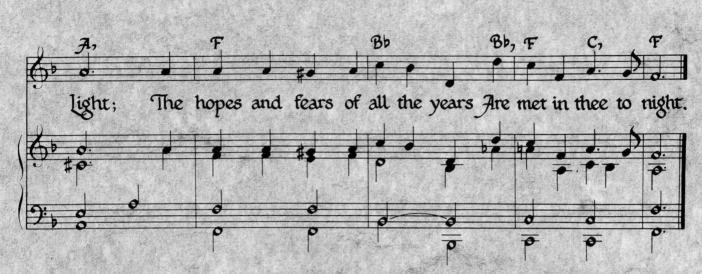

Light; The hopes and fears of all the years Are met in thee to night.

2. For Christ is born of Mary,
   And gathered all above,
   While mortals sleep, the angels keep
   Their watch of wond'ring love.
   O morning stars, together
   Proclaim the holy birth,
   And praises sing to God the King,
   And peace to men on earth!

3. How silently, how silently,
   The wondrous gift is giv'n!
   So God imparts to human hearts
   The blessings of His heav'n.
   No ear may hear His coming,
   But in this world of sin,
   Where meek souls will receive Him still,
   The dear Christ enters in.

4. O Holy Child of Bethlehem,
   Descend to us, we pray;
   Cast out our sin and enter in;
   Be born in us today!
   We hear the Christmas angels
   The great glad tidings tell;
   O come to us, abide with us,
   Our Lord Emmanuel!

"A Christmas Carol" *See Dickens, Charles.*

Charity *See Goodwill.*

Children

New toys, flying reindeer, elves, twinkling lights, candy canes—these magical symbols of Christmas are especially associated with children. More so than any other holiday, Christmas is a child's time of year. Who else awaits the holiday with such impatience? When Santa Claus loads his sleigh, jounces over roof tops, and squeezes down chimneys, it's for the children. When the stockings are hung and the dollhouses are assembled, it's for the children. And when the star-shaped sugar cookies and popcorn garlands mysteriously disappear, we all suspect the children.

Youngsters figure prominently in the literature of Christmas as well. Clement C. Moore wrote "A Visit From St. Nicholas" for his own little ones. It was a little boy, author Truman Capote himself, who told of his elder cousin's fruitcakes and kites in *A Christmas Memory*. And who could forget Tiny Tim's earnest prayer, "God bless us, every one!", in *A Christmas Carol?*

These days, Christmas wouldn't be Christmas without the produced-for-children-but-loved-by-all television classics "Rudolph the Red-Nosed Reindeer," "A Charlie Brown Christmas," and "How the Grinch Stole Christmas." Children even have their own seasonal songs, among them, "The Chipmunk Song" and "All I Want for Christmas (is my two front teeth)." And who doesn't envy the little girl who meets Kris Kringle in the movie *Miracle on 34th Street?*

Christmas is a time for children in countries all over the world. In fact, most of the traditional celebrations center on the youngsters. For example, Mexican children look forward to striking at the piñata, a decorated container filled with candy and gifts. In Denmark, children hear about Juul Nisse, elfin figures who help with chores but also cause trouble.

Finally, it is the children who add sparkle to the most routine of holiday events, from the proud little tykes leading the Christmas parade to the nervous ones at the mall, waiting to sit on Santa's knee. Though it might be argued that the season is really "for kids from one to ninety-two," there's truly something special between Christmas and the little ones. After all, it was a child who inspired the holiday in the first place. *(See also International Christmases; Television; Music, Christmas; Movies; Poems and Stories; Santa Claus; Stockings; Toys.)*

Charlie Brown and the Peanuts gang have delighted children since the 1950s. Perhaps one of cartoonist Charles Schulz's best-loved creations is the television production of **A Charlie Brown Christmas.**

Calendars for Grandparents

Every year right after Christmas, the year changes, and everyone all over the world has to get a new calendar. You can buy one, or you can try making one. Home-made calendars made by children make great Christmas presents for moms, dads, and grandparents, to mention a few.

Most calendars have a page for every month. Engagement calendars usually have a page, and sometimes a picture for each week. Some calendars have only one picture for the whole year with a pad of pages at the bottom showing the months and days. Other calendars are just to look pretty and have a picture for each month but no days at all.

Home-made calendars can be of any variety, but children do best with twelve pictures at most. Very young children may only hold together for four or even one picture. They can make one picture for each season if twelve monthly pictures loom too large. It is possible to purchase both large and small unillustrated calendars at the stationer's. These can be pasted on below the pictures, saving eons of time in production and avoiding the possibility of setting dates on the wrong day of the week. Or a child may prefer to make a calendar with only illustrations and no dates at all. (Be aware that most children like to make things that look "real" and real calendars have dates.)

The calendar crafts that follow are simple to make and will provide year-round enjoyment for a proud grand-parent or other relative. The Calendar with Pictures and Days is the type gen-erally given away by businesses to their clientele around the holidays. The Wall and Desk Calendars are even easier to make, since they only require pictures. With the wall type, the pictures hang down in a long chain of months. The desk type sits atop a little stand.

CALENDAR WITH PICTURES AND DAYS

Materials:
13 pieces of posterboard or other stiff paper 8½ inches by 11 inches (or larger or smaller)
paper punch
rubber cement or white glue
2 Chinese jacks (available in toy stores)
crayons, paint, or colored papers for the pictures
a pad of one-month calendar sheets for *next* year

1. Punch two holes in one sheet of posterboard on one long side. Using the first sheet as a pattern, punch holes in all 13 sheets.

2. Make a hole in the very center of the top of each page to hang the calendar up.

3. To make the pictures, write the name of one month on each sheet, lightly, in pencil, keeping the two holes at the bottom of the sheet. Do this for all 12 months. Then start with the month you're in and think about what happens in your family and your town during that month and use that as a basis for the illus-trations. Be sure the single hole is at the top when you make the pictures. Poster paints and felt-tip markers work best because they don't smear. Craypas and Crayons are okay, but little bits may stick to the calendar part. You can also cut or tear paper into figures and make a collage pic-ture for each month, cut pictures from magazines, or paste in photos of your family for each month. If the pages get wavy from the paint or the glue, press them flat afterwards under a pile of books.

4. Stack your calendar in reverse order, December through January. Put the extra page on top of December. Slip the Chinese jacks, or little pieces of string, through the two holes. Turn the calendar over, and open the first page: Your January picture should be on top, with a blank back of February at the bottom.

5. Buy one-month calendar sheets to fit your pictures, or draw them your-self, being careful that the numbers fall on the right days of the week for next year. They are different each year.

6. Using either rubber cement* or a little white glue, spread very thin very quickly, paste January's calendar under January's picture (on the back of February's picture), and so forth. The thirteenth sheet will only have December's calendar sheet on it. On the back of January's picture, make the cover. The cover can say what-ever you want: "Nana's Calendar" 1992, or you can draw another pic-ture on it. The two holes should be at the top when you draw it.

*Note: Rubber cement is the best glue to make a flat bond, but it is also toxic if you inhale too much. Keep your nose away from it. Be sure there is plenty of ventilation and you are working in a fairly large room. **Never let very young children use rub-ber cement.**

Rubber cement works a little like Velcro: both sides have to be glued. Smear a thin layer on both surfaces you want to stick together. Let them dry. If you are gluing something large, like a calendar sheet, place two unglued strips of cardboard, or paper, on top of the bottom sheet to keep the two surfaces separate. Carefully position the top sheet where you want it, then slide the two strips out, and press the top sheet in place, starting in the center of the paper. Once the two layers are together, you will never again get them apart. If there are bits of rubber cement outside the area to be glued, you can rub them off afterwards with your finger.

DESK CALENDAR

Materials:

13 sheets of stiff paper. Plain
4- by 6-inch index cards are ideal.
(If you have three 8½- by 11-inch
sheets of posterboard left, you can
carefully cut them in quarters and
use a piece of construction paper for
the cover.)
paper punch
crayons or paints for pictures
2 Chinese jacks (or a little string)
cardboard for stand: 3 pieces 4¼ by
6 inches

1. Decide whether you want your pictures wide or tall. Then punch two
   holes about 2 inches apart in what
   you decide is the top of each card.
2. Draw the cover, and the pictures,
   writing the name of the month on
   each picture.
3. Stack the pages in order and put
   rings through the 2 holes.
4. Make a little stand by taping the
   cardboard pieces together to look
   like a pup tent. Lay the calendar
   over it with pages hanging down on
   both sides. If you want an easier
   package to wrap, don't tape the last
   seam of the stand. Let the person
   who gets it do that.

WALL CALENDAR
·········

Materials:
13 sheets of stiff paper. Plain
    4- by 6-inch index cards are ideal.
    (If you have three 8½- by 11-inch
    sheets of posterboard, you can care-
    fully cut them in quarters and use a
    piece of construction paper for the
    cover.)
paper punch
crayons or paints for pictures
24 Chinese jacks (available in toy
    shops), or a long piece of string

1. Decide whether you want your pictures to be wide or tall. Then punch
   2 holes about 2 inches apart in
   what you decide is the top of each
   card and 2 in the bottom of each
   card, matching the holes as you go
   to make sure they align perfectly.
2. Draw the cover, and the pictures,
   writing the name of the month on
   each picture.
3. Using the 24 little rings or string,
   string the cards up to make a long
   chain, then fold the chain up like
   an accordion with the cover on top.

*Here are some picture ideas for
both calendars:*

January: New Year's Day, skating, sledding, snow, coming to school with new
clothes on, drying mittens.

February: Valentine's Day, skiing,
snowmen, getting firewood from the
woods, ice racing, playing hockey, ice
fishing, George Washington's and
Abraham Lincoln's birthdays.

March: Snow melting, making
maple syrup, birds flying north, mud,
kite flying, Lent, daffodils and crocuses,
spring cleaning.

April: Easter, daffodils, baby
lambs and goats, baby chicks and rab-
bits, planting gardens, catching fish.
In the south: trees leafing out, cherry
blossoms.

May: Baby leaves on the trees,
tulips, planting gardens, fish swimming
upriver, baby wild animals, wild birds
nesting, baby ducks, mosquitoes, brush-
ing out animals' winter coats.

June: School's out, mowing the
lawn, going fishing, fresh vegetables in
the garden, visiting grandparents, sailing, swimming.

July: Fourth of July, butterflies,
parades, swimming, playing outside, pic-
nics, American flags, sailing, playing
with the fire hydrant or the hose.

August: Sailing, swimming, fishing,
working, summer camp, camping out.

September: School busses, school,
apples, books, new clothes, splitting
firewood, a big full moon.

October: Pumpkins, Halloween,
leaves turning colors, washing windows, hunting geese and ducks, putting up storm windows, putting boats
in storage for winter, Thanksgiving
(Canada).

November: Thanksgiving (U. S.),
raking leaves, trees are bare, winter
clothes, making Christmas presents,
deer hunting, baking.

December: Woodstoves, Christmas.

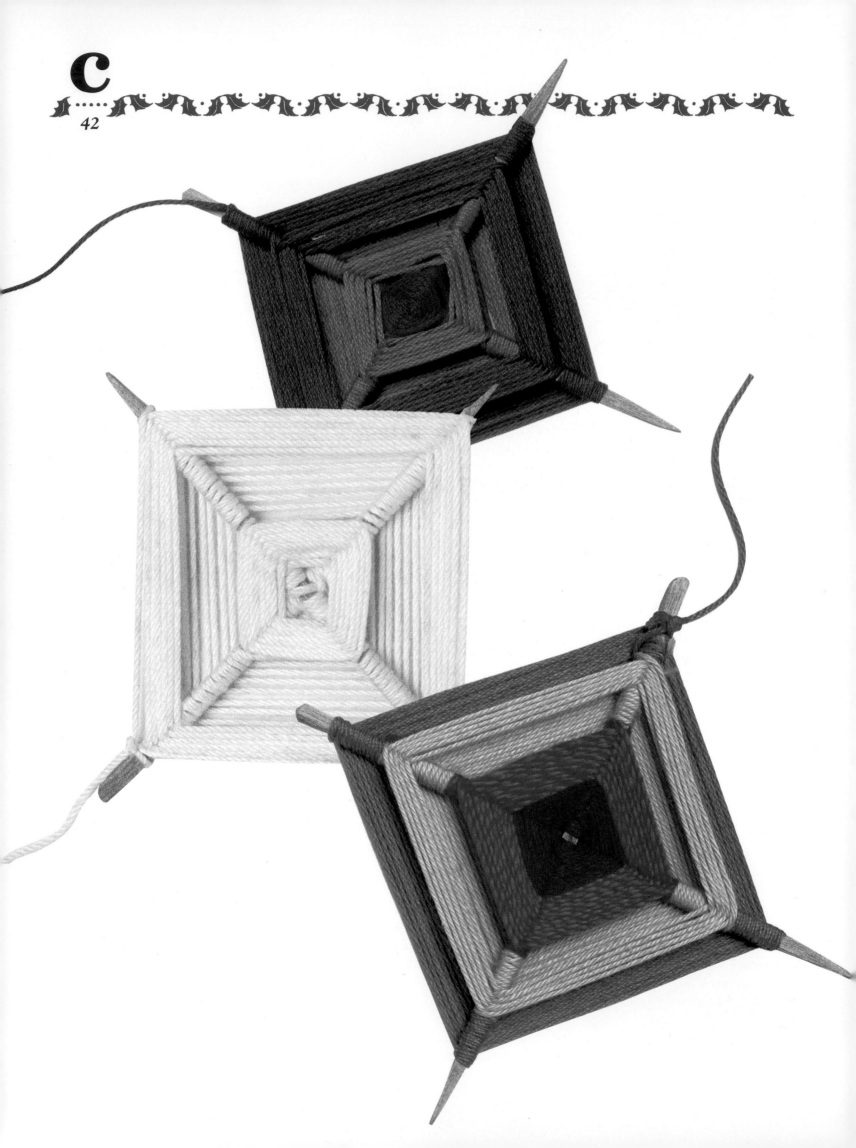

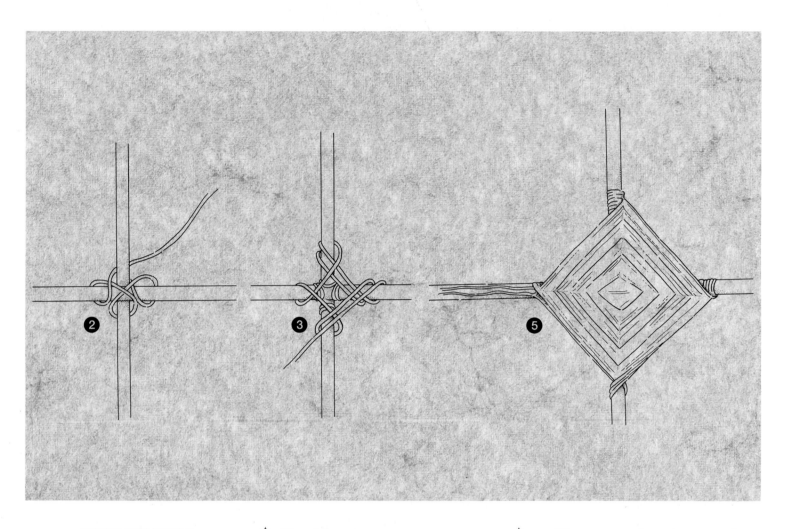

OJOS DE DIOS

Ojos de Dios (*ohos* day *dee*-ohs) are a favorite children's craft project, because they're pretty and easy to make. Ojos de Dios, which means Eyes of God, in Spanish, originally come from the Mediterranean, where young girls make them as decorations for springtime. In the United States, they are used as decorations any time of year, but especially to give a little Spanish flavor to the Christmas tree.

Ojos de Dios are fun to make and look striking on the Christmas tree. They can be made with a pair of sticks of almost any size. Even children who never make anything can learn the simple winding pattern that forms the smooth or indented yarn surface.

✦ **Materials:**
Small or large toothpicks, or smooth, even sticks of any size up to about 8 inches. Young children do best with larger sticks.
Brightly colored scraps of embroidery thread or silk for tiny ojos, scraps of knitting yarn for larger ojos.

1. Hold sticks in the shape of a cross.
2. With first color, wrap end of the thread as shown in order to hold sticks together. Or wrap twice in each direction around the cross.
3. Begin wrapping sticks, moving 90 degrees clockwise, as shown. Pull up snugly each time, being careful not to overlap threads and not to pull the cross out of shape.
4. For a variation, turn the Ojo de Dios over and wrap on the back side.

This creates a three-dimensional effect. To space the thread out a little, as on the white ojo, wrap the yarn around each stick once more before going to the next stick.
5. To change colors, snip the thread leaving a 1-inch tail, and lay it against the stick. Put the tail of the new color in the same place, wrap the new color around the stick, then continue wrapping from stick to stick, covering both tails each time you come to that stick. Hold both tails in place until they are well-anchored. Snip the ends off after four rounds.
6. To finish, tie a knot around one stick with the remaining thread, and place a drop of white glue on the knot. The tail is used as a hanger.

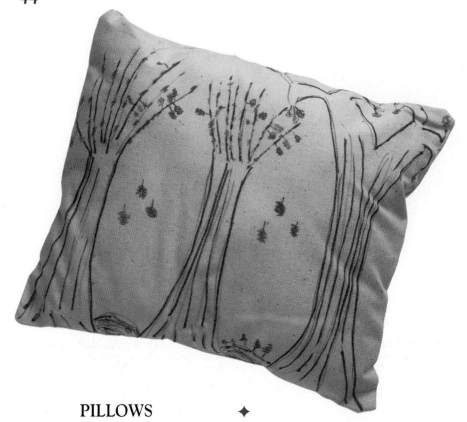

PILLOWS

Throw pillows and kneeling pillows are great home-made Christmas gifts for a family to make. Adults can make lovely creations in cross-stitch, needlepoint, bargello, and patchwork. Children can make all manner of pillows: fuzzy, brightly colored, round, big, small, and some with drawings on them. No matter how simple they are, they are useful, and their unique designs are treasures.

The instructions below are for a pillow created by a very young child. However, an adult must help with some of the work. These instructions can be expanded indefinitely to any kind of material and even to varied shapes.

Materials:
1 or more permanent markers, with
    bullet tips for easy drawing
2 pieces unbleached muslin, about 12
    inches square
piece of corrugated cardboard,
    12 inches square or larger
straight pins
thread to match the muslin
sewing machine
1 small package polyester stuffing

1. Adult cuts two matching squares of muslin; pins one square to the corrugated cardboard. The child draws a picture on one of the muslin pieces. Remove cardboard.
2. Adult pins both pieces together, picture side in, and stitches around, leaving a ⅜-inch seam allowance and a 6- to 8-inch gap through which to stuff the pillow.
3. The child then stuffs pillow, using lots of stuffing, almost the whole bag. Make sure to stuff the corners.
4. Adult then stitches the gap closed.

✦ *Christmas*

The word Christmas comes from the early English phrase *Christes Masse,* which means Christ's Mass. Christmas is the day on which Christians celebrate the birthday of Jesus Christ. Although there is no documented evidence of the birth of Jesus, Christians in many countries observe it on December 25. The story of Jesus's birth is told in the *New Testament,* in the first two chapters of Matthew and Luke.

Christmas also has a history that predates Jesus's birth. For many centuries, cultures have stopped work for a midwinter festival. This is the time of year when the hours of sunlight gradually begin to lengthen, and consequently, when the growing season begins again. Saturnalia, the Roman festival honoring the gods of seeds and sowing, and *Dies Solis Invicta Nati,* the holiday of the followers of Mithras, the Iranian god of the sun, were typical of these December festivals. It was not until the fourth century A.D. that the birth of Christ was officially celebrated, and though the date fluctuated somewhat in those early years, it seemed natural for the holiday to fall in the season of rebirth.

Christmas and the weeks preceding it mark the happiest and busiest time of the year for millions of Christians all over the world. They celebrate the season by exchanging gifts and cards, decorating their homes with trees and other greenery, preparing and eating traditional foods, giving and attending parties, visiting with family and friends, extending goodwill to needy persons, singing Christmas carols, and attending church.

WISHING YOU A MERRY CHRISTMAS

WITH THE YEAR'S BLESSING IN ATTENDANCE.

Copyright.

Some Christmas customs, such as gift-giving and attending church, are directly related to the story of Jesus's birth. Yet the observance of the holiday is not always religious in nature, at least not directly. Excess intake of alcohol and feasting at parties and the commercialization of gifts, for example, are strongly criticized for their antispiritual purposes.

Unlike any other religious holiday, however, Christmas brings much of North America and Europe to a virtual standstill. Most businesses are closed, so that employees may spend the day with their families—opening gifts, celebrating, and attending church. In fact it is not uncommon for work to stop during the nine days that span Christmas to New Year's Day. Although Christmas is a Christian celebration, it has become a Western experience.

Christmas Eve

For all practical purposes, the role of Christmas Eve in the Yuletide festivities is just as big as that of Christmas Day. In the oldest Christian calendars, Christmas Eve was known as Adam and Eve day to celebrate the belief that Christ had by his sacrifice wiped out the burden of their sin. In medieval times, Christmas Eve was considered the night of the vigil of the Nativity and thus, the most hallowed of the season. On this night, the head of the family rolled the heavy Yule log into the hearth and set it afire, and at the stroke of midnight animals were said to gain the power of speech.

Holiday traditions all over the world commence on Christmas Eve as

well. In Ireland the large red Christmas candle surrounded by holly sprigs is lit on Christmas Eve and set in the front window to symbolically guide the Holy Family to shelter. Children in most countries hang their stockings or leave their shoes on the hearth on Christmas Eve to be filled with presents during the night.

In Italy elaborate nativity scenes are constructed and erected on Christmas Eve and dismantled on Epiphany, January 6. Armenians eat fried and boiled spinach on Christmas Eve because they believe the Virgin Mary ate boiled spinach on the night before Jesus was born. In countries where Christmas is still essentially a religious festival—such as Italy, France, Spain, and Belgium—the Christmas

St. Francis of Assisi is often credited with having originated the nativity scene when he arranged a setting with live animals. Representations of holy settings were constructed everywhere in Europe during the Middle Ages. The tradition continues in America today.

"At Christmas play, and make good cheer, For Christmas comes but once a year." —Thomas Tusser, **Five Hundred Points of Good Husbandry (1557)**

Eve midnight mass is a central part of celebrations.

The day before Christmas is frequently treated as a holiday in North America today, although it usually depends on what day of the week Christmas falls on. In any case, the evening itself is always a time for celebrating. Some families open their gifts on Christmas Eve and enjoy a big dinner; others wait until Christmas Day; and still others extend the gift-giving from Christmas Eve throughout Christmas Day and enjoy festive dinners. It is a time for last-minute shopping, parties, hanging up stockings, and tucking children into bed with visions of sugarplums dancing in their heads. (*See also December 25; Christmas; International Christmas.*)

Colors, Christmas

Red and green are the traditional colors of Christmas. The holly plant, with its green leaves and red berries, is thought to be the inspiration, but otherwise, there does not seem to be any historical or legendary reason for the association of red and green with Christmas. Dark blue, white, silver, and gold have inexplicably become recognized as secondary color choices for the season.

Commercialism

The literal meaning of Christmas may be "Christ's Mass," but in recent years it has also become a time for consumerism. Modern-day celebrators seem more concerned with getting and spending than the story of Jesus's birth. Decorations are not only likely to be expensive, but many of them feature nonreligious symbols such as candy canes and toy soldiers. For most, it's hard to imagine Christmas without an excess intake of food and drink. And many a manufacturer and retailer works the whole year through in order to clear a big profit during the holidays. We even have shops that sell nothing but Christmas items as well as amusement parks with Christmas themes.

Complaints about the growing commercialism of Christmas are frequently heard, yet this year-end indulgence actually predates Christmas itself. Almost every civilization throughout the ages has celebrated the time when winter starts to wane, the sun starts to climb in the sky, and crops and fruits

are reborn. The early Romans called this festival Saturnalia after Saturn, the god of farming, and it was celebrated with wild feasting throughout the Roman Empire. The Greek Libianus wrote of it: "The impulse to spend seizes everyone. He who the whole year through has taken pleasure in saving and piling up his money becomes suddenly extravagant."

Over time, Saturnalia-type festivals came to be merged with the Church's celebration of Jesus's birth. So when people complain that Christmas isn't what it used to be, the fact of the matter is that spending, eating, and drinking are actually part of the holiday's history. (*See also Shopping, Christmas; Shops, Christmas; Places, Christmas; Saturnalia.*)

Cracker, Christmas

When the colorful cardboard tube of a cracker is pulled apart, it produces a small popping noise and a

party favor from inside. Today, crackers containing confetti are seen at birthday parties, but to children of the Victorian age, a cracker, or snapper, was an important part of the Christmas celebration.

An Englishman named Tom Smith is credited with creating the original Christmas cracker in the 1860s—he got the idea from a French candy (bonbon) that was wrapped in colored tissue paper and had to be tugged by two children before it burst open. By 1900 the manufacture of crackers—filled with miniature jewelry, crowns, flowers, books, toys, and masks—had become a minor industry. For the children of the rich, stores sold crackers three feet long that spewed forth multiple prizes with a big bang. In England, the Christmas cracker as a party favor is still an important part of the Yuletide table setting.

December 25

There is no evidence of the exact date of the Nativity, and almost every month has been suggested by different scholars. The story of why most Christians observe Christmas on December 25 is complicated at best.

Early Christians did not believe that Christ was born divine, but that he attained divinity when he was baptized by John the Baptist at age thirty. Even Jesus's followers did not celebrate his birthday, fearing it would put Christ on par with King Pharoah, who did celebrate his birthday.

By the third century of the Christian era, scattered groups were celebrating the event at various dates. Many, for example, believed that Jesus's spiritual and physical birth occurred on the same day, January 6, the feast of

✦ Epiphany. December 25 was finally selected in the fourth century, when St. Cyril of Jerusalem requested that Pope Julius I settle the matter once and for all. It was about that time that the Church first acclaimed Christmas as a public festival.

· Today in the United States, Christmas Day is a federal legal public holiday. If December 25 falls on a Sunday or Saturday, the federal holiday is usually observed on the following Monday or the preceding Friday. Families traditionally gather on December 25 to exchange gifts and share their happiness, although for many, December 24 is reserved for some or all of the festivities. Church services are also held on Christmas Eve and Christmas morning. (*See also Christmas; Christmas Eve; The First Christmas; Epiphany; Saturnalia.*)

Decorations and Decorating

The tradition of decorating with evergreens and candles is older than Christmas itself. The Romans, for example, decorated with garlands of evergreens in celebration of Saturnalia, the winter feast. The evergreens symbolized eternal life because they survived winter. Candles have lighted holy days since the beginning of recorded time; Saturnalia celebrations frequently included lighted candles to symbolize that Christ was the Light of the World.

Today we continue to decorate the halls with boughs of holly, trees, wreaths, mistletoe, and other evergreens. Candles still have a place among our December decorations, too—in fact, Christmas candles now come in every way, shape, and form, and have inspired electric lights.

Glass Christmas balls are enchanting on a tree, but they can also be used to make other decorations. Arrange three or four amidst the greenery on a mantle. Attach a few to your front-door wreath, or let them glisten in a glass bowl.

Besides electric lights, there is a vast collection of other, "new" Christmas symbols. Stars and Santa Claus, for example, frequently appear among today's holiday decorations. Unlike pine cones or sprigs of holly, stars and Santas couldn't be gathered in the woods and so they were first created by hand—as a glass-blown ornament, for example. Eventually, they were manufactured, taking on forms as diverse as plastic life-size Santas for the lawn and giant stars to crown Christmas trees in town squares. These days manufactured decorations are commonplace; handmade and natural arrangements, or a unique assemblance of the manufactured, are the most rare and sought after.

Decorating Made Easy

- Carefully select the locations for your decorations, and do not plan too many for a room.
- Arrange silver balls on a silver tray for an effective centerpiece. To keep the balls from rolling around, add a few pieces of evergreen.
- Weight the corners of a festive tablecloth with bells. Fasten tiny bells to the corner of each cloth napkin, too.
- Place red and green soap balls at every bathroom sink.
- Fill a large bowl or other attractive container with fruits and vegetables in seasonal colors. Mix bright red apples

with green apples or limes; use pomegranates, red onions, red and green cabbages, and Brussels sprouts in any combination.

- Pine branches in an old stoneware crock or tin watering can make a dramatic display on a side table or in front of the hearth. To hold the branches in place, fill the container with sand or kitty litter. Replace the branches as they fade.
- Transform a simple kitchen shelf with a fragrant topiary rosemary tree, a lace-edged napkin, and shimmering gold balls arranged alongside a pretty cream pitcher.
- Fill flowerboxes on the porch or at the window with sprays of evergreens or berries on branches mixed together.
- Group angels made of any and every

material—pottery, china, wax, wood, glass, brass—on a mantel, windowsill, or table. Arrange evergreen boughs around them.

- Add ornamental balls of various sizes and colors to a cellophane box in which a corsage was received. Tie the box with a red satin ribbon and place on a foundation of greens and berries.

- Set a festive mood in the kitchen. Create a still-life of candles arranged with an assortment of metal cooking utensils: cookie cutters, steamers, molds, graters. Add cinnamon sticks, ribbon, and sprigs of holly. When the candles are lit they'll create a warm glow—just be sure to keep the holly away from the flame.

- To create a country atmosphere, place a woven table runner on a long trestle table. Then arrange glossy magnolia leaves, pine, holly, fruit, and a pair of

✦ *Anyone can create a magically pretty Christmas scene with a few choice elements and a little imagination. Put sprigs of green around wall hangings and chandeliers. Mound apples, lemons, oranges, grapes, pineapples, and pine cones in pretty bowls. Improvise with snowflake like doilies, red and green ribbons, and ornaments of all types.*

duck decoys on top as decorations.
- Gild pinecones and nuts to adorn a centerpiece or wreath. You'll find supplies at well-stocked art-supply stores.

✦ **Storing Decorations**
- Remove all fresh plant materials from wreath bases before storing, otherwise they will dry and crumble. Replace with fresh evergreens next Christmas. Cover each wreath, swag, or other hanging decoration with a plastic bag and hang on a hook.

- Put all Christmas ornaments in one box, ribbons in another. Separate heavy, ornate decorations and light, delicate ones in different boxes.

- Wrap figurines individually in tissue paper or newspaper. Pack them in their own boxes with the heaviest ones on the bottom.

- Wrap candles individually in wax or cellophane paper. Lay flat in a box.

- Place tissue paper between folds of a tablecloth to prevent wrinkles.
(*See also Ornaments; Tree, Christmas; Stars; Candles; Evergreens.*)

HEART BASKETS

Here is a wonderful Christmas decoration that symbolizes the joy of the holiday season. In Scandinavian countries, woven heart baskets of wood shavings or paper filled with candy and raisins adorn the Christmas tree. But they can also be hung on doorways, from pegboards, from knobs on kitchen cabinets, and anywhere that they can brighten the home at Christmas.

Heart baskets are good to weave on the cozy, long evenings near the winter solstice in Denmark. Weaving them takes up whole evenings for Scandinavian families, and adults play with complicated and fanciful weaving patterns, sometimes producing bells, little hearts or other symbols within the woven pattern, while children learn by manipulating simpler forms.

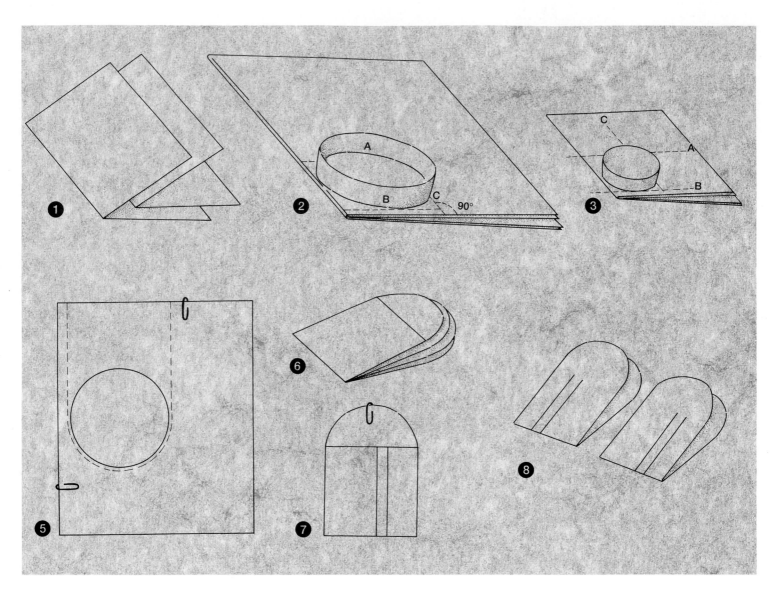

Materials:
2 sheets paper, 8 by 10 inches,
 in two different colors
jar lid or other circular object
scissors
paper clip
glue

1. Fold two pieces of paper together in half.
2. Place a jar lid or other disc so that it almost touches the fold and one edge. Mark the paper at points A, B, and C.
3. Draw a line lightly from the edge of the paper through point C and extend it a little longer than the

diameter of the jar lid. Make sure it's square (90 degrees) with the edge of the paper. Use the corner of a piece of paper or a triangle.
4. Lightly draw a line (perpendicular, 90 degrees, to the fold) through point A and extend it just beyond the line marked C. This will make a square.
5. Move the jar lid so that the center lines up with the corners of the square along line C and trace around the part outside the square.
6. Cut out the shape, clipping the layers together with a paper clip to prevent them from slipping.

7. Make one or more cuts from the fold to about 1/8 inch beyond line C of the square—just beyond where the square meets the semicircular top. These should be perpendicular to the fold.
8. Turn the outside layer inside out so that the pencil marks are on the inside. The cuts should be mirror images of one another.
9. With the round ends toward you, begin weaving in the middle. Weaving is inside-outside, not over-under.
10. Weave As first, then Bs, then Cs. The fold of the Cs are the point of the heart.

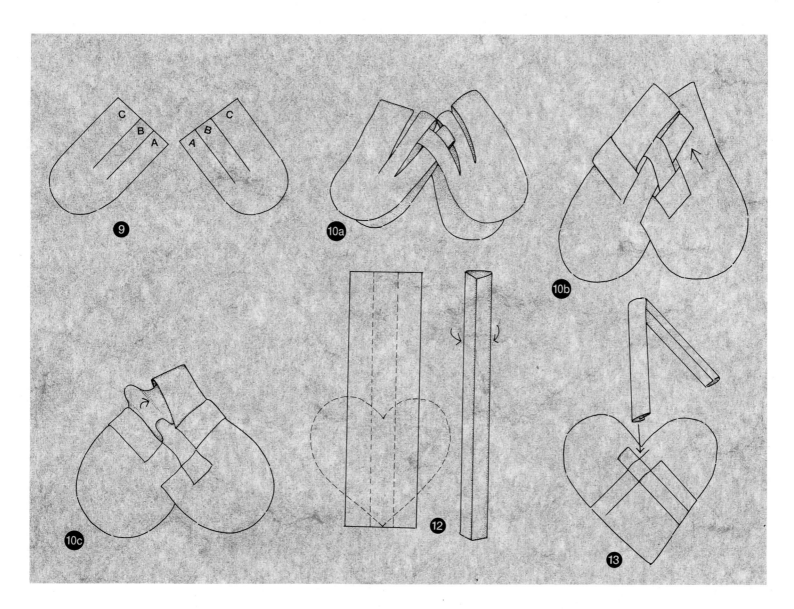

11. If you do it right, the two sides of the heart will pull apart to form a basket. If they don't, check to see if one or more strips are woven over-under instead of inside-outside. Either toss the heart and start over, or carefully pick it apart and re-do it.

12. Cut a paper strip at least twice as long as the heart is high and half as wide as one side of the heart. Fold as shown, lengthwise then crosswise.

13. Glue one end between the two layers on each side of the heart.

14. Fill with candy and hang on Christmas tree or anywhere else that seems appropriate. Do not expect the candy to be there the next day.

✦ **Suggestions:**
• Make no more than one or two cuts on your first try so that you can understand the principle before you try something complicated.
• After you've made one heart, try arranging the cuts differently, making equal strips or narrow and wide strips. Even numbers of cuts make an odd number of weaving strips, and one color will predominate. Odd numbers of cuts make an even number of weaving strips and the colors will be equally divided.
• There are many wild and wonderful effects to be achieved by experts in heart weaving. If you get good at it,

✦ consider these tips:
• Properly placed half circles on the cuts, facing the center of the weaving, can make the shape of a little heart within the larger heart basket.
• Other images can be produced on the centerline by engineering the cuts as half silhouettes. This does take engineering.
• Angles and curves can be worked into the cuts, creating interesting visual effects from radiating pop-art checks to fish scales. Again, a precise engineering mind is the key. Men and women alike love to show off their skill at this in Scandinavian countries.

During his time, clergyman Samuel McChord Crothers was known for the quality of his writings on a multitude of subjects. An essayist for the Atlantic Monthly, Crothers also published a number of stories and books, among them, Miss Muffet's Christmas Party *(1901)* and The Children of Dickens *(1925)*.

Dickens, Charles

Although Charles John Huffam Dickens may be best-known for his story about Ebenezer Scrooge and the ghosts that haunted him, *A Christmas Carol* is only one of five books with Christmas themes credited to the English novelist. Following the publication of *A Christmas Carol* in London in 1843, Dickens turned out one holiday-warmer after another: *The Chimes* (1844), *The Cricket on the Hearth* (1845), *The Battle of Life* (1846), and *The Haunted Man* (1848).

Dickens was also widely celebrated for many of his other works, among them, *Great Expectations* (which begins with a Christmas feast), *Oliver Twist*, *David Copperfield*, and *A Tale of Two Cities*. But at Christmastime, it's Scrooge and his infamous oath, "Bah, humbug!" that makes Charles Dickens a household name. Today, *A Christmas Carol* is broadcast on television several times each season in different versions—from films that closely follow the original storyline to Americanized, modernized, even cartoon adaptations.

Dickens was a Christmas symbol of sorts during his own time, too. In fact, this English novelist is credited with reviving his country's interest in celebrating the holiday, since many customs, such as carols and caroling itself, were virtually forgotten during the economic upheaval of that period. Experts claim it is no coincidence, for example, that the first Christmas cards were produced in the 1840s. Dickens, who was born in 1812 and died of a stroke in 1870, must have been pleased by the influence he had, since he once stated that his purpose was to leave his mark on the celebration of Christmas. *(See also "Bah, humbug!"; Carols; Movies; Poems and Stories; White Christmas.)*

Dieting

No other season sabotages more healthful diets than Christmastime, since so many Thanksgiving-through-New Year's events center on rich foods and so many North Americans are concerned about their health. Here are some tips on how to eat wisely during the holidays:

- When baking, substitute margarine for shortening or butter; evaporated skim milk for evaporated milk or cream; skim milk for whole milk; egg whites for whole eggs; nonstick spray coating for butter or oil.
- To tame your hunger, eat a healthful snack such as whole-grain crackers or fruit before attending a party. When you arrive, stay close to the vegetable tray, away from the meat, cheese, and dessert spreads.
- Don't drink too much alcohol—it is not only high in calories itself, but overindulging can lead you to go against your better judgment, and cause you to overeat. Sip slowly, or better yet, substitute mineral water with a squirt of citrus or a "cocktail" of seltzer or fruit juice.
- You don't have to pass up your favorite foods at the family's annual Christmas dinner—but you don't have to go overboard either. Eat lightly and healthfully throughout the day, then at dinnertime, put only small servings of dressing, ham, deviled eggs, and the other high-calorie selections on your plate.
- If dessert is important to you, then cut back even more during dinner. Keep in mind that sweets made with nuts, eggs, butter, cream, and cream cheese are most likely to be fattening.
- Exercise. If it's a white Christmas, sledding, skiing, and ice-skating are wonderful activities. Instead of focusing on eating, spend time with family members by taking a walk. Even the calories expended in small workouts here and there—by parking a distance from the mall, carrying your own groceries to and from the car, finding and cutting your own Christmas tree—will add up fast.

Drinks to Warm You at Christmas

Here are recipes for several traditional holiday drinks.

GLOGG

peel (with zest) of ½ orange, cut in
    julienne strips
1 cup raisins
½ cup whole blanched almonds
3 crushed cardamom pods
3 crushed coriander seeds
2 cinnamon sticks
10 whole cloves
2 cups water
1 gal. domestic port wine
1 fifth cognac
1 pint bourbon
½ pint rum
4 tablespoons sugar
½ orange, sliced thin
whole cloves

Place the first seven ingredients in a
large stockpot, add the water, and simmer for 30 minutes. Then add the next
five ingredients, heating until just
below the boiling point. Carefully light
the surface of the glogg with a match,let
it burn a few seconds, then extinguish
by placing a lid on the pot. Serve warm
in a punch bowl, with a few orange
slices studded with one or two cloves
floating on top.
Serves 24 to 30

HOT MEXICAN CHOCOLATE

2 tablets Mexican chocolate
¼ cup water
2 quarts milk
whipped cream
cinnamon

Gently melt chocolate tablets in water
over very low heat. When chocolate is
dissolved, add milk, stirring and heating
until just under the boiling point.
Remove from heat, and pour into a jug
or pitcher. Beat with a whisk until foamy
(or use the traditional tool, a *molinillo*).
Serve topped with whipped cream and a
dash of cinnamon, if you like.
Serves 6 to 8

HOT MULLED WINE

1 cinnamon stick
4 whole cloves
½ teaspoon grated nutmeg
1 tablespoon sliced lemon peel (zest
    removed)
½ cup sherry
1 bottle red wine
sugar to taste

Place the spices and lemon peel in a
large saucepan, barely cover with water,
and simmer for 30 minutes. Strain, and
add the sherry, wine, and sugar. Heat
but do not boil.
Serves 6

EGGNOG

6 eggs, separated
½ to ¾ cup sugar
2 cups heavy cream
2 cups milk
2 teaspoons vanilla or rum extract
grated nutmeg

In a large bowl, beat the egg whites until
stiff but not dry, gradually adding sugar.
Beat the yolks in another large bowl
until they are lemon yellow. Fold in the
egg whites. In a third bowl, beat cream
until stiff, then add it to the eggs along
with the milk and flavoring, stirring.
Chill. Sprinkle with grated nutmeg
before serving. (The eggnog may need a
gentle stirring before serving.)
Serves 8

ROMPOPE de CALABAZA
(Pumpkin Eggnog)

6 eggs, separated
½ cup sugar
½ cup pumpkin puree
2 pints half-and-half
¼ cup Jamaican rum

In a large bowl, beat the egg whites until
stiff but not dry, gradually adding sugar.
Beat egg yolks in another large bowl
until pale lemon yellow. Beat pumpkin
into egg yolks, then fold in the egg
whites. In a third bowl, beat the half-
and-half until frothy. Add it to the mixture along with the rum. Stir to blend.
Serve very cold.
*Note: For the adults, add 2 cups rum,
cognac, or whiskey to the nog.*
Serves 6

Electric Lights

See Lights, Christmas.

Elves

The idea that Santa has elfin helpers is probably related to ancient Northern European folklore. Scandinavians have long believed in small, magical men called *tomten*, or *julenisser*. Viking farmers thought that these small, bearded creatures helped protect them from evil. In order to ensure a prosperous year, farmers offered food to the elves to keep them happy. Later, this pagan belief was Christianized, and the julenisser became bearers of holiday gifts in the popular imagination. These days they are believed to do helpful things like cleaning up the kitchen, making a batch of cookies, bringing in

✦ wood from the barn, and keeping the fire going in the fireplace.

If the family is good to the elves, leaving them a bowl of rice pudding or other dessert on Christmas Eve, the elves do even more important things like reminding the family to unplug the iron before leaving for a party, to blow out a candle, or put the screen in front of the fireplace before going to bed. These are things people ordinarily forget when they are busy—as they are at Christmastime—so it's good to have a few julenisser around the house. The helpful elves that live with Santa at the North Pole are no doubt first cousins to ✦ the julenisser.

ELVES ON SKIS

✦ These elves are made of pipecleaners, spruce, wooden beads, scraps of yarn, and bright red felt. Their hair is inch-long frayed bits of yellow, synthetic rope.

Because their faces aren't painted on, they could be smiling or sad, depending on how kind their families have been to one another. They can be made by adults or children, or by both together.

The skis are made of scraps of split ash from basketmaking, wetted and held in place until they set, but can also be made of veneer purchased in a small roll ✦ at the lumberyard, hobby shop, or doll-house supply store.

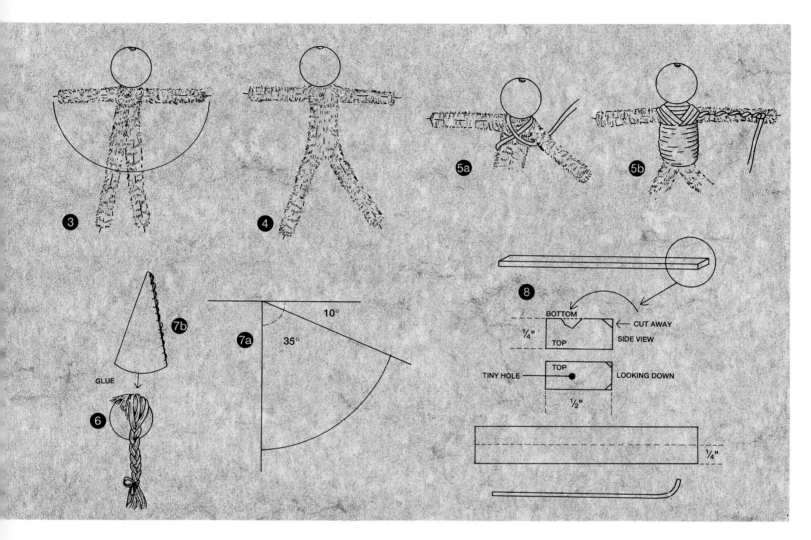

Materials for one elf:

¾-inch natural-colored or pink bead

12-inch red pipecleaner

small amounts of leftover yarns in two colors

1 square inch of red felt for hat

1½ square inches red felt for skirt

red thread

1 inch long piece of ¼ by ¼ inch spruce (from model airplane hobby shop)

3 to 4 inches by ½ inch veneer or thick split ash (basketry or seating material) about ¹⁄₁₆ inch thick

small bits of hair-colored synthetic cord or yarn

scissors

white glue

1. Cut pipecleaner in two.

2. Bend one half and jam into hole in bead.

3. Attach arms by knotting other half of pipecleaner under glass bead.

4. Twist the pipecleaner in step two to form a torso and legs.

5. Starting at the shoulder, wind the yarn over itself to lock in the tail, and then keep winding until the body is fat enough. Then continue winding yarn around the arms. Leave room at the end of each arm for the hands. Wind the yarn back towards the neck, loop it tightly around the shoulders and torso in an X, knot it, and dab a spot of white glue on the tip of the yarn to hold it in place.

6. Glue strings of yarn onto the bead to make the hair.

7. For the hat, cut a triangle with a curved base from red felt, as shown in illustration. Sew the ends of the triangle together to form the hat.

8. Make shoes by cutting away small chinks from the corners of spruce. Drill a tiny hole in the top of each piece of spruce.

9. Cut skis from the veneer or split ash. Dunk the skis under water to dampen them, then bend the ends upwards as in the photograph, and hold them until they set (about five minutes).

10. Glue the feet onto the skis. Put a dot of glue into the holes on top of the shoes, and insert the ends of the pipecleaner legs into the holes on the shoes, and hold the elf up until the glue sets.

Epiphany

Also known as Twelfth Night, Little Christmas, or Old Christmas, Epiphany is a holy day celebrated in Roman Catholic, Anglican, Eastern European, and other Christian churches on January 6. The date is now used to designate the visit of the three wise men to the holy child, but before the fourth century, January 6 was honored as representative of both the birth and baptism of Jesus. These important manifestations of Jesus's deity, in fact, give January 6 its official name, since Epiphany means "manifestation."

In the Catholic calendar, Epiphany is an entirely distinct holiday from Christmas, and lasts from January 6 to January 13. Throughout the years other countries have honored Epiphany with various customs. During the time of Queen Elizabeth I, for example, Twelfth Night was observed in England with wild celebration. This custom died out, but special church services are still held on the date. (*See also Wise Men.*)

"In winter, when the snow lay glittering on the ground, a hare would often come leaping along, and jump right over the little Tree. Oh, that made him so angry! But two winters were past, and in the third the Tree was so large that the hare was obliged to go around it."
—*Hans Christian Andersen (1805–1875)*, **The Fir Tree**

Evergreens

The custom of decorating homes and churches with evergreens began in ancient times. The Romans exchanged green tree branches for good luck on the first day of January, and the English borrowed this custom for Christmas. An old English rhyme stated: "Holly and ivy, box and bay, put in the church on Christmas day."

Holly, ivy, boxwood, and bay are only a few of the wide array of evergreens symbolic of Christmas. Pines, spruces, and firs are used for Christmas trees, as well as wreaths. Mistletoe was a folkloric and medicinal plant before it became so closely associated with the holidays, but we know it best when it's suspended over a festive doorway.

Rosemary fell out of popularity during the nineteenth century, but at one time these attractive, scented gray-green leaves were a Christmas favorite. The plant was believed to have acquired its scent when Jesus's swaddling clothes were hung over it.

The stiff, linear leaves of yew and

the fragrant oval leaves of bay, or laurel—used to wreathe the brows of Roman heroes—also had a prominent place among Yuletide greenery, but now they are seldom seen. Holly, with its shiny leaves and bright red berries, is the staple favorite today.

Decorating With Evergreens

• To extend the lives of greens, don't cut them until the night before you plan to use them. Cut carefully with clean, sharp shears so that the wounds heal quickly. Crush the cut ends of the boughs and place them in a pail of cold water overnight. The greens will absorb enough water to keep for a week or so.

• Bundles of mixed evergreens are obtainable from most nurseries at Christmastime. If these evergreens are not available in quantity, buy two Christmas trees and cut up the extra branches for wreaths, swags, and garlands.
(*See also Mistletoe; Holly; Ivy; Trees, Christmas; Wreaths.*)

Family

Christians in North America place more emphasis on the family at Christmas than at any other time of the year. For many, to be away from home at Christmas is unheard of. Popular songs ("I'll be Home for Christmas") and movies (*The Homecoming— A Christmas Story*) demonstrate the importance of spending the holidays with one's most long-standing acquaintances in one's most familiar surroundings.

The emphasis on family tradition stems from America's earlier days, when immigrants weren't able to bring much material wealth to their new country but did bring the richness of their cultures. These traditions and rituals were used to mark all important events in the life of the family, from the birth of a child to death of an elder.

After World War II, families became increasingly fragmented by mobility and divorce, and traditions in some families fell by the wayside. For these people, psychologists recommend that family traditions be reinstated or at least created. These rituals establish a sense of belonging (especially for children), unite generations, and reemphasize the spiritual side of celebrations.

Some family traditions are similar from home to home. For example, families usually decorate the tree together in the weeks or days preceding December 25. Parents select and prepare gifts from Santa Claus in secret, then place these toys or other desirables around the tree before their children awake on Christmas morning. On Christmas Eve or Christmas Day, families typically gather to open gifts from each other and to share at least one meal.

Other family traditions are less traditional. Ancestry frequently plays a part in homes at Christmas—for example, a family might gather on a Saturday in December to prepare *nisu*, a traditional Finnish bread requiring many hours of work. Another family might gather on Christmas Eve to trim the tree or watch family movies. Children may be encouraged to put on a concert or to act out a skit. The important thing, say experts, is to uphold some old customs while creating a few new ones. This way, your family gatherings will offer something for everyone, young and old, in the Christmas spirit.

Any time, any place, any family, Christmas sets the stage for picture-pretty traditions. Etching at right: "Hoisting the Union Jack," by Alfred Hunt, **Illustrated London News**, *December 1876*

"The Fir Tree"
See Poems and Stories.

The First Christmas (The Christmas Story)

Most of the Christmas story comes from the first two chapters of Luke and Matthew in the New Testament. Other information and suppositions, such as the belief that Mary rode a donkey from Nazareth to Bethlehem and the names of the three Wise Men, have been supplied by historians through the ages.

The two New Testament accounts are brief and have only one thing in common:

that Mary and Joseph were in Bethlehem when Jesus was born. Yet the details from these varying texts complement each other and have been molded into the one story that Christians know by heart.

Mary and Joseph
The gospel of Luke tells how an angel appeared to Mary. Even though she was a virgin, the angel said, Mary would soon give birth to a son, whom she would call Jesus. "He will be great and will be called the Son of the Highest: and the Lord God shall give unto him the throne of his father David." (Luke 1:32)

In Matthew, an angel appears to Joseph, the man that Mary is engaged to. After learning that Mary was pregnant,

"They found Him in a manger;
Where oxen feed on hay;
His Mother Mary kneeling down,
Unto the Lord did pray."
—God Rest You Merry Gentlemen (1770)

Joseph had decided to break the engagement secretly so as not to disgrace her publicly. But the angel tells him in a dream: "Joseph, thou son of David, fear not to take unto thee Mary thy wife; for that which is conceived in her is of the Holy Ghost." (Matthew 1:20) Joseph did as he was told.

It is in Luke that Joseph takes Mary from the town of Nazareth, in Galilee, to the town of Bethlehem, in Judea, where King David was born. A descendant of David, Joseph went there to register for the census. But while they were there, the time came for Mary's child to be born. Since there was no room at the inn, Mary laid her firstborn, wrapped in swaddling clothes, in a manger.

The Shepherds and the Angels

At that same time there were some shepherds nearby who were taking care of their flocks. When an angel appeared to them, shining "Round about them" with "the glory of the Lord," they were afraid. But the angel said to them, "Fear not: for, behold, I bring you good tidings of great joy, which shall be to all people. For unto you is born this day in the city of David a Saviour, which is Christ the Lord. And this shall be a sign unto you; Ye shall find the babe wrapped in swaddling clothes, lying in a manger." (Luke 2:10-12)

And suddenly a great army of angels appeared and sang, "Glory to God in the highest, and on earth peace, good will toward men." (Luke 2:14)

When the angels went away, the shepherds decided among themselves to go to Bethlehem to find Mary, Joseph, and the baby. When they did, they told them what the angels had said. Then the shepherds returned, singing praises to God for all they had heard and seen, for it had been just as the angel had told them.

The Wise Men and King Herod

The story of the Wise Men comes from Matthew. During the time when Herod was king, some men who studied the stars came from the east to Jerusalem and asked, "Where is he that is born King of the Jews? for we have seen his star in the east and are come to worship him." (Matthew 2:2)

When King Herod heard about this he was very upset, so he called together his chief priests and teachers, and asked them where this King was to be born. The priests and teachers answered that the scriptures foretold of the Messiah's birth in Bethlehem.

So Herod called the Wise Men to him and asked about the exact time the star appeared. Then he sent them to Bethlehem with these instructions: "Go and search diligently for the young child, and when ye have found him, bring me word again, that I may come and worship him also." (Matthew 2:8)

The Wise Men left and followed the star until they came to the place where the child was. They were so joyous that they fell to their knees to worship the baby and gave him gifts of gold, frankincense, and myrrh. Before the Wise Men left, God warned them in a dream not to return to Herod, so they returned to their countries by another road. *(See also Wise Men; Star; Nativity Scenes.)*

Food

As a traditional Christmas activity, eating is second only to exchanging gifts—and eggnog, fruitcake, and plum pudding are holiday symbols. Libraries and bookstores are teeming with seasonal cookbooks, and nearly every family has a special dish or mealtime tradition that Christmas wouldn't be complete without.

History

The winter feast can be traced back almost as far as history itself. As winter set in and fodder was in short supply, it became necessary to slaughter livestock and preserve it for use toward the end of the barren season. Thus economic necessity and the spirit of sacrifice were merged.

In medieval times, kings dined on gilded peacocks. First the feathered skin was stripped off, then the bird was roasted, sewn back into its skin, and the beak was gilded. Henry III ordered festivities in York in 1252 that included the slaughter of 600 fat oxen. Early settlers in Australia put braised kangaroo into their plum pudding, and smoked elephant and fried locusts were served at at least one holiday dinner attended by hunters at Koba on the White Nile. Christmas dinner at Voisin's in Paris during the Prussian siege of 1870 included elephant consommé, braised kangaroo, and roast cat garnished with rats. Of course, these examples are extreme, but demonstrate that Christmas fare throughout the ages has not always been classic lamb, turkey, or goose.

In North America today families usually gather on Christmas Eve or Christmas Day for a meal not unlike the traditional Thanksgiving feast: turkey, one of the few seasonal foods from the New World itself, is likely to be served with stuffing, candied sweet potatoes, pumpkin pie, cranberry sauce or relish, fruitcake, and myriad side dishes.

Yet in some homes ham is the centerpiece of the Christmas feast—perhaps because the pig is the boar's relative, and in the history of many countries the boar was the favored sacrificial animal. A popular seasoning for the Christmas ham is a combination of pineapple, cloves, and brown sugar.

There are many international culinary traditions that have contributed to North American holiday festivities, yet each region adds its own favorites to the Christmas menu, too. In Louisiana, for example, the Christmas meal might include seafood from the nearby coast and Creole seasonings, a tradition passed down from the French who originally settled there. On the West Coast, the holiday menu tends to feature local agricultural specialties, such as artichokes and citrus fruits, as well as Spanish and Mexican fare. *(See also International Foods.)*

TRADITIONAL CHRISTMAS EVE DINNER

Roasted goose is a classic Christmas dish. This dinner draws on old-fashioned fare, such as Date Plum Pudding, and enlivens the table with rich and seasonal colors.

Roasted Goose with Chestnut and
    Fruit Stuffing
Whole Yams with Candied Ginger
    Topping
Red and Green Christmas Salad with
    Vinaigrette
Date Plum Pudding
Serves 8 to 10

ROASTED GOOSE

1 8- to 10-pound goose
1 lemon
Chestnut and Fruit Stuffing (optional,
    can be made separately)

1. Preheat oven to 425 degrees F.
2. Remove any excess fat from the cavity of the goose. Rub the inside with juice from the lemon. If you are cooking stuffing with the goose, pack the stuffing into the cavity.
3. Place the goose on a rack in an uncovered pan. Bake for 15 minutes, then turn heat down to 350 degrees F and cook 3 to 3½ hours (allow about 25 minutes per pound), until juices run clear. Baste goose once in awhile with its own juices and pour off excess fat. Goose may splatter a lot, so open oven door carefully.
4. Allow to cool about 20 minutes before carving. Remove stuffing.

CHESTNUT AND FRUIT STUFFING

4½ cups shelled chestnuts*
1 stick unsweetened butter
¾ cup minced celery
¾ cup minced onions
½ cup light cream
½ cup dry sherry
2 cups dry unseasoned breadcrumbs
¼ cup raisins
¼ cup chopped dried apricots
1½ teaspoons salt
1 teaspoon black pepper

1. If chestnuts are not tender enough to puree, simmer them for 5 to 10 minutes until tender. Puree and set aside.
2. In a heavy-bottom skillet, melt butter. Add celery and onions and cook until vegetables are soft, about 7 minutes. Stir cooked vegetables into pureed chestnuts.
3. Add all remaining ingredients and mix well. If cooking stuffing separate from bird, bake in a greased baking dish at 350 degrees F for 30 minutes.

*To shell uncooked chestnuts: Cut a cross gash on their flat sides. Cover them with boiling water and simmer for 20 minutes. Drain and remove shells and inner skin.

WHOLE YAMS WITH CANDIED GINGER TOPPING

The ginger topping can also be used with boiled yams or tossed with peeled quartered yams before they are baked.

8 to 10 whole yams
½ cup crystallized (candied) ginger
1 stick butter at room temperature
½ cup brown sugar

1. Preheat oven to 375 degrees F.
2. Wash yams, pierce with fork or knife, and bake for 45 to 60 minutes, until tender.
3. Mash ginger with fingers or a fork. Blend ginger, butter, and brown sugar together well. Split each yam open lengthwise on the top and fill loosely with 1 to 2 tablespoons of ginger mixture.

RED AND GREEN SALAD WITH VINAIGRETTE
· · · · · · · · ·

Salad:
1 small head arugula
1 small head radicchio
½ head redleaf lettuce
1 bunch watercress
1 small sweet red pepper, cut into thin
    strips

Vinaigrette:
¼ cup balsamic vinegar
2 tablespoons white wine vinegar
1 clove garlic, bruised
6 sun-dried tomatoes, chopped
2 tablespoons minced fresh Italian
    parsley
1 tablespoon Dijon mustard
1 teaspoon sugar
½ teaspoon salt
⅔ cup olive oil
freshly ground black pepper

1. Wash and break arugula, radicchio,
   and lettuce into bite-size pieces.
   Toss with watercress and red pepper
   in large salad bowl.
2. To make the vinaigrette, combine
   vinegars, garlic, tomatoes, parsley,
   mustard, sugar, and salt. Set aside for
   30 minutes at least, then stir in oil.
   Toss dressing with salad just before
   serving. Add freshly ground pepper
   to each serving.

BAKED DATE PLUM PUDDING
· · · · · · · · ·

The original plum pudding, reportedly
invented by a cook for William the
Conqueror in the eleventh century,
actually had plums in it. (Another legend says that Daga, the Druid god of
plenty, first concocted this fragrant,
spicy, and darkly rich "cake.") This
"mess in an earthenware pot" evolved
with the substitution of prunes and then
other dried fruits for the plums. It is also
often made in the oven as well as
steamed on the stove top.
Makes 1 loaf

½ cup butter
⅔ cup brown sugar
6 eggs
½ cup raisins *and/or* currants
1 cup chopped dates
2 cups fresh breadcrumbs
½ cup flour
⅔ cup coarsely chopped walnuts *or*
   pecans
2 teaspoons cinnamon
½ teaspoon cloves
½ teaspoon nutmeg
½ pint heavy cream, whipped with
   1 teaspoon vanilla

1. Preheat oven to 375 degrees F.
   Grease and flour a loaf pan.
2. Cream butter and sugar together.
   Beat in eggs one at a time.
3. In a separate bowl, combine all
   remaining ingredients, except for
   cream. Stir dry ingredients into wet
   ingredients, mixing just until
   blended. Pour into prepared pan.
4. Bake for 40 to 50 minutes, until a
   cake tester inserted in center comes
   out clean. Serve hot, or cool thoroughly before wrapping and storing
   in refrigerator. This cake keeps for
   months.
5. To serve, wrap loaf in foil and reheat
   in a 300-degree F oven for about 30
   minutes. Top each serving with
   whipped cream.

*Note: You can also soak this cake in rum,
brandy, or sherry. See Step 4 of Brandy-
Scented Pecan Fruit Cake, page 107, for
instructions.*
Makes 1 loaf

CLASSIC MIDWINTER DINNER

Serve this wonderful dinner on Christmas Day. It uses foods especially in season in midwinter—many of which, such as cranberries, are classically North American.

Roasted Marinated Quail
Polenta with Wild Mushrooms
Hot Winter Greens with Pancetta
   Dressing
Root Vegetable Puree with Glazed
   Cranberries
Persimmon Pudding with Lemon
   Sauce
Serves 8

ROASTED MARINATED QUAIL

Keep in mind that you must begin preparing the quail 24 hours in advance.

Marinade:
1 cup white wine
¾ cup olive oil
juice of 1 whole lemon
½ cup chopped parsley
3 tablespoons fresh thyme *or* 1 tablespoon dried thyme
2 tablespoons crumbled dried sage
4 cloves garlic, minced
1 teaspoon juniper berries
2 teaspoons salt
2 teaspoons black pepper
16 quail
6 to 8 tablespoons butter

1. Combine all ingredients but quail and butter for marinade. Split birds down back and flatten. Marinate at least 24 hours (or up to 48 hours) in the refrigerator in a glass or enamel dish with cover. Turn birds occasionally to distribute marinade.

2. Preheat oven to 375 degrees F. Remove quail from marinade and reserve marinade (for Polenta with Wild Mushrooms, which follows). In a heavy skillet, sauté quail in butter until lightly brown, about 7 minutes.

3. Transfer sautéed quail to roasting pan and place in oven. Roast for 10 to 12 minutes, just until juices begin to run clear.

POLENTA WITH WILD MUSHROOMS

Before you begin this recipe, keep in mind that the mushrooms must be soaked in water for an hour before they are cooked. The polenta can be prepared three days before the meal.

Polenta:
9 cups cold water
2 teaspoons salt
1 cup stoneground cornmeal
2 cups coarsely ground cornmeal *or* polenta
1 cup grated pecorino romano cheese

For the mushrooms:
1 ounce dried porcini (soaked in enough water to cover, for one hour)
4 tablespoons butter
½ pound mixed wild mushrooms, such as hedgehog, chanterelles, shiitake, oysters, sliced
½ pound of button mushrooms, sliced
reserved marinade from quail

1. To make polenta, bring 6 cups water and salt to a boil. Combine both cornmeals with 3 cups cold water and slowly stir into boiling water. Lower heat and cook mixture, stirring continuously, for about 20 minutes, until very thick. Stir in cheese and blend well. Cool slightly.

2. Pour polenta into 1 or 2 loaf pans and pat down. Allow to cool for 20 minutes and firm up before slicing. (You can cover polenta and refrigerate for up to 3 days in advance. If you do so, reheat in a 350-degree F oven for about 25 minutes.)

3. To prepare the mushrooms, drain porcini in a colander and rinse, making sure they are free of any grit. Chop coarsely.

4. Heat butter in a heavy skillet and add all mushrooms. Cook until lightly browned, about 7 minutes. Pour in marinade from roasted quail and turn up heat. Cook until marinade is slightly reduced, about 7 minutes. Serve mushrooms and sauce over quail and polenta.

HOT WINTER GREENS WITH PANCETTA DRESSING

1 pound collard greens, washed and chopped
1 pound Swiss chard, washed and chopped
1 pound spinach, washed and chopped

Dressing:
4 thin slices pancetta bacon, diced
½ cup olive oil
¼ cup balsamic vinegar
½ teaspoon salt
½ teaspoon sugar
½ teaspoon crushed red pepper

1. In a large pot, steam collard greens for 20 minutes. Add chard and steam another 10 minutes. Add spinach and steam another 3 minutes.

2. To make the dressing, blanche the pancetta in boiling water for 2 minutes. Drain and sauté in 2 tablespoons of the olive oil. Combine pancetta with remaining ingredients.

3. Toss cooked greens with dressing and serve immediately.

GLAZED CRANBERRIES

1½ cups water
1 cup sugar
3 cups cranberries

1. Combine water and sugar in a saucepan and cook until sugar is dissolved.

2. Stir in cranberries and cook over moderately high heat until liquid is slightly reduced. (You can prepare glaze up to 3 days in advance. If you do so, store covered in the refrigerator and reheat before using.)

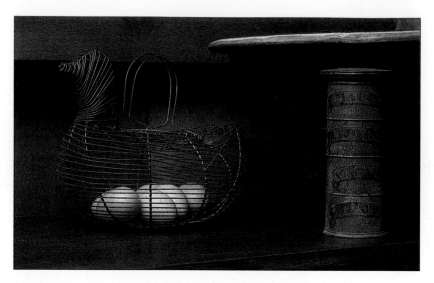

ROOT VEGETABLE PUREE WITH GLAZED CRANBERRIES

To simplify cooking preparations on Christmas Day, you may wish to make the cranberry glaze up to three days in advance.

2 cups large diced celery root
4 cloves garlic
1 large rutabaga (about 2½ pounds), peeled and cut into 1-inch chunks
3 medium-size potatoes, peeled and quartered
3 medium-size turnips, peeled and quartered
1 cup milk
4 tablespoons unsalted butter
2 teaspoons salt
1 teaspoon black pepper
Glazed Cranberries (recipe precedes)

1. In a 4- to 6-quart pot combine celery root, garlic, rutabaga, potatoes, and water to cover. Cook until vegetables are slightly tender, about 15 minutes. Add turnips and cook another 7 to 10 minutes, until they are tender.
2. Drain cooked vegetables and puree with milk, butter, salt, and pepper until creamy. Top each serving with a heaping tablespoon of Glazed Cranberries.

♦ PERSIMMON PUDDING WITH LEMON SAUCE

This delightful pudding can be prepared as much as a week before Christmas. The sauce that accompanies it can be made three days in advance.

2 cups pureed persimmon
3 eggs
½ cup milk
2 teaspoons vanilla
2 tablespoons Triple Sec (optional)
½ cup dark brown sugar
⅔ cup of flour
1 teaspoon baking soda
½ teaspoon salt
1 teaspoon cinnamon
¼ teaspoon nutmeg
¼ teaspoon ground ginger
Lemon Sauce (recipe follows)

1. Preheat oven to 350 degrees F.
2. Beat together persimmon, eggs, milk, vanilla, Triple Sec, and sugar.
3. Sift together remaining ingredients. Stir dry ingredients into persimmon mixture and mix just until blended.
4. Pour into a greased baking dish and bake about 30 minutes, or until pudding tests done with a cake tester.
5. Serve hot or cold with warm Lemon Sauce. (This pudding can be made up to 1 week in advance. Store covered in the refrigerator, and reheat before serving.)

♦ LEMON SAUCE

¾ cup fresh lemon juice
grated zest from 1 lemon
½ cup sugar
4 egg yolks, beaten
4 tablespoons butter, cut into 4 to 6 chunks

1. Combine lemon juice, zest, and sugar in a saucepan and heat until sugar is dissolved.
2. Stir some of the hot lemon liquid into beaten egg yolks and slowly stir back into saucepan. Cook sauce over low heat, stirring continuously, until it is thick enough to coat a spoon.
3. Stir in butter chunks. Remove sauce from heat. Stir sauce until butter melts.
4. Serve over pudding. (You can make sauce up to 3 days in advance. Cool before storing, covered, in there refrigerator. Reheat over low heat.)
Makes about 1¼ cups

HERB-AND-SPICE BRUNCH

Here is a hearty brunch that includes a lively mix of dishes. Herbs and spices make these recipes especially memorable.

Roast Leg of Lamb
Wild Rice with Herbs and Pine Nuts
Stuffed Miniature Pumpkins
Glazed Brussels Sprouts and
    Chestnuts
Sage Onion Rolls
Baked Wine-Glazed Pears with
    Spiced Crème Fraîche
Serves 8 to 10

ROAST LEG OF LAMB

At Christmas, lamb is served in countries such as Iceland, Spain, and Sardinia. And in New Zealand, the leg is stuffed and called a "colonial goose." Keep in mind that for this recipe, you must begin preparing the lamb at least two days in advance.

7½ pound leg of lamb, boned
8 to 10 cloves of garlic, sliced
3 cups dry red wine
1 cup olive oil
3 tablespoons dried rosemary, crumbled
2 teaspoons salt
1 teaspoon freshly ground black pepper
½ cup flour

1. With a sharp knife, pierce deep slits throughout lamb and insert slices of garlic. In a large baking dish or non-reactive metal pan, combine all remaining ingredients, except for flour. Marinate lamb for 2 to 3 days, covered, and refrigerated, turning a few times.

2. Preheat oven to 325 degrees F. Bake lamb for 1½ to 2 hours, until meat thermometer reads 180 degrees F. Baste often with marinade.

3. Place strained pan juices with enough remaining marinade to equal 2 cups in a saucepan. Stir in flour and cook over moderate heat until thickened. Spoon this gravy over individual servings.

WILD RICE WITH HERBS AND PINE NUTS

4 tablespoons unsalted butter
½ cup chopped onions
1 stalk celery, minced
½ pound mushrooms, sliced
1 tart apple, cored and finely chopped
2 cups long grain wild rice
4 cups stock
½ cup pine nuts
½ cup chopped mixed fresh herbs if available (mint, parsley, marjoram, sage, tarragon) or ¼ cup herbs if dried
salt and pepper to taste

1. Melt butter in a saucepan. Add onions and celery and cook for 7 minutes. Add mushrooms and apple and cook 3 minutes longer. Stir in rice and cook for 5 minutes over moderate heat.
2. Stir in stock, cover pot, and cook 25 minutes, or until rice is tender and liquid is absorbed. Stir in nuts and herbs. Taste and adjust seasonings.

GLAZED BRUSSELS SPROUTS AND CHESTNUTS

2 pounds brussels sprouts
4 tablespoons unsalted butter
1¼ cups peeled roasted chestnuts
salt and freshly ground pepper, to taste

1. Add brussels sprouts to a saucepan filled with boiling water and cook until tender, about 10 to 12 minutes. Drain.
2. In a heavy-bottom skillet, melt butter. Cook butter, stirring with a whisk or wooden spoon, just until it begins to brown. Reduce heat. Stir in chestnuts and cook for 3 minutes. Stir in brussels sprouts and cook another 3 minutes, stirring constantly. Season to taste. Serve immediately.

SAGE ONION BUNS

Sage and onion are two complementary holiday flavors that distinguish this moist, yeasted egg dough.

1 package dry yeast
¼ cup warm water
1 medium onion, chopped
4 tablespoons butter
¼ cup chopped fresh sage or 2 table-spoons dry sage
1 stick softened butter
3 tablespoons sugar
4 eggs
2 egg yolks
½ cup warm milk
5 to 6 cups flour
2 egg whites beaten with 2 teaspoons water

1. Dissolve yeast in water.
2. Cook onions in four tablespoons of butter until soft, about 7 minutes. Stir in sage.
3. In an electric mixer, cream stick of butter, sugar, eggs, and yolks. Stir in yeast, milk, and sage-onion mixture.
4. Mix in enough flour to make a stiff dough. Knead dough for 10 minutes, until smooth and satiny. Place in a bowl in a warm spot to rise until double in bulk, about 1 hour.
5. Punch down dough and knead again. Taking egg-size portions of dough, shape into rounds and place on greased baking sheets. Allow to double in bulk again, about 45 minutes. While dough is rising, preheat oven to 325 degrees F.
6. Brush rolls with egg-white-and-water mixture. Bake for 15 minutes, until bottom is lightly golden.
Makes 2 dozen

MINIATURE PUMPKINS STUFFED WITH CURRANTS AND NUTS

Some ingredients of this recipe must marinate overnight, so begin preparations the day before your brunch.

½ cup brandy
½ cinnamon stick
¼ cup currants
8 miniature pumpkins
fresh juice of 1 whole orange
2 tablespoons brown sugar
8 tablespoons chopped walnuts
½ stick butter

1. Combine brandy, cinnamon, and currants and set aside to marinate overnight.
2. Preheat oven to 325 degrees F. Slice off tops of pumpkins and clean out seeds.
3. Add orange juice and brown sugar to currant mixture. Distribute mixture among pumpkins. Add 1 tablespoon walnuts to each pumpkin. Divide butter evenly among pumpkins, placing a pat on top of mixture.
4. Bake for 30 to 35 minutes, until pumpkins are tender.

BAKED WINE-GLAZED PEARS WITH SPICED CRÈME FRAÎCHE

Pears are in peak ripeness in most areas around the holidays. If fresh mint leaves are available, top each serving with a sprig to enhance the holiday preparation.

10 firm-ripe Bosc or Bartlet pears with stems intact

2 cups Zinfandel wine

½ cup sugar

1 cinnamon stick

5 whole cloves

1¼ cups crème fraîche mixed with ½ teaspoon cinnamon and ¼ teaspoon cloves

1. Preheat oven to 400 degrees F. Trim bottom of pears so they stand up. Peel pears, but do not remove stems.
2. In a 2- to 2½-quart baking dish combine wine, sugar, cinnamon, and whole cloves. Set pears upright in dish, spooning mixture over pears.
3. Bake for 45 minutes, basting pears occasionally with wine mixture. Serve warm or cold with a dollop of crème fraîche and a couple spoonfuls of wine syrup.

Frankincense

According to the story of the first Christmas, three wise men came to the infant Jesus and presented him with gifts from their homelands. Balthasar, King of Ethiopia, brought frankincense in a censer—a jar used in religious ceremonies—to symbolize the child's divinity. Frankincense, also known as olibanum, is a fragrant gum resin obtained from certain Asian and African trees of the genus *Boswellia*. Since ancient times, it has been burned as an incense during religious services. (*See also The First Christmas; Gold; Myrrh; Wise Men.*)

Gifts

The giving of gifts at Christmastime is as old as Jesus's birthday itself and is probably symbolic of the Wise Men's presentation of gold, frankincense, and myrrh. Legend has it that shepherds and peasants offered gifts at the manger as well. But it is just as likely that the tradition is borrowed from the Roman Saturnalia, when people gave gifts of money, precious metals, or sweets to the poor and needy.

History

It was not until the mid-nineteenth century that North Americans began giving gifts to friends and family, instead of just to the disadvantaged. Although throughout Europe the tradition of Christmas presents dates back to the sixteenth century, North Americans may have held back on giving gifts to one another because English colonists were accustomed to providing clothes, special rations of food, and trinkets for their workers, servants, and slaves at Christmas as part of Christian piety, commonplace since the Middle Ages. Gifts were not given at Christmas to friends and family.

The concept of Christmas gifts as we know it today did not exist until the mid-nineteenth century, when retailers first recognized the marketing potential of gift-buying. Before then nearly every gift was made at home. Christmas gifts were more popularly known as holiday gifts or New Year's gifts, perhaps because gift-giving used to be common on the first day of the year in some countries.

In England, for example, tenants and peasants were expected at the beginning of the year to give small samples of the fruits of their labor to the lords of the manor, who reciprocated with something more valuable. Some countries—France, for instance—still exchange gifts on New Year's, but most of the English- and German-speaking countries now favor Christmas Day. When merchants in nineteenth-century New York began to commercialize Christmas as the time to buy gifts, the idea quickly became a traditional seasonal activity.

Ideas

Though store-bought gifts are certainly the norm in this country and time, handmade ones are just as feasible and in some cases preferred. For the person who has everything, is hard to please, or who simply would cherish a cheerful tin of homemade cookies or a red-ribboned basket of pinecones from you, creativity is the answer.

In North America and England, gifts are placed beneath the tree. But in Germany, useful or practical presents are laid on a near-by table. The Christmas tree in Germany is intended to be solely a thing of beauty.

Services also make fine gifts. A car wash, babysitting, or prepaid visits to the hairdresser, masseur, photographer, personal trainer, or optician would be welcomed by most any recipient.

Gifts that don't quite fall into the store-bought or handmade categories include potted plants and fresh-cut flowers, pets, magazine subscriptions, dinner at a restaurant or at home, or just time spent together doing favorite things, like seeing a movie or a show, going to the beach, or playing tennis. Whenever a gift isn't suitable for wrapping—dancing lessons or future tickets to a ballgame, for example—make your own special certificate or coupon.

A handmade gift, of course, is a natural when economics are a consideration. You can also stretch your dollar by shopping all year-round. Since linen traditionally makes a good gift, white sales in January and August will afford you some savings. Golf, tennis, and camping equipment is sale-priced in September and October; ski and skating items are reduced in March and April. Coupled with the arbitrary sales of other great gifts—clothes, accessories, books, music, videotapes, stationery, frames, kitchen supplies, personal appliances— the possibilities are diverse.

Buying in advance is the answer to the lack-of-time problem as well. Don't hesitate to pick up a surefire gift

even though it's May and you're not on an "official" shopping trip. Whenever possible, give the same gift to more than one person—funky socks for all your nieces, for example, or a wine made in your state for all of your long-distance friends. Thanks to the abundance and variety of mail-order houses today, it's even possible to trim

shopping down to a few phone calls.

For many the biggest problem with gift selection is knowing *what* to give. One of the most efficient ways is to keep a dossier for everyone on your list all through the year. Whenever you hear "I've always wanted a charm bracelet" or notice that someone's shaving kit is on its last legs, that's your cue to write it down.

Outside of the obvious suggestions—toys for children, house gifts for the homeowner, food or scented soap for the older person—a rule of thumb is to consider the personality of the gift recipient. Some of us prefer basic, practical gifts, such as calendars and electric blankets; others love to receive something a little extravagant, something they'd never buy for themselves, and comes as a total surprise. What that might be is up to your imagination.

Gift Wrapping

A collection of beautifully wrapped presents beneath a tree is one of the quintessential images of Christmas. By all means, do not restrict yourself to traditional giftwrap, but consider other possibilities: wallpaper, fabric, handmade writing papers, and unusual boxes make lovely and surprising coverings for gifts. Even something as simple as plain brown wrapping paper can work as a beautiful canvas for hand-painted touches and pretty stickers.

Consider also working small three-dimensional objects into your gift-wrap designs. Tuck a toy soldier into the fold of a ribbon; add a cluster of jingle bells to the center of a bow; or simply adorn your gifts with perfectly preserved dried roses attached by ribbons or bows.

Sending Gifts

If you won't be hand-delivering your gift, you must consider packaging logistics. Soft goods (clothes, linen) need a self-supporting box or tear-resistant bag. Pack liquids (cologne, vinegars, syrups) in a secondary container, surround them with absorbent packaging, and then place them in a box with a leak-proof interior. Make sure powders (cornmeal, fragrance) are sift-proof by securely closing their lids or openings. Perishables (food) should be packed in absorbent cushioning. Fragile items (clocks, frames, stemware) should be cushioned to distribute shocks; use foam plastic or padding. Odd-size items (posters, racks) require fiberboard tubes or boxes with length not over ten times the girth; cushioning should consist of preformed fiberboard or foam plastic shapes.

If more than one gift goes in a box, wrap each item individually with enough padding to prevent damage from shock. Separate wrapped items from outer package surfaces with padding or foam plastic. Pressure-sensitive filament tape is preferable for sealing, but reinforced tape is permitted.

Address labels should be legible from thirty inches away. Include the zip code and be sure to put the return address on the inside of the box as well as the outside. To prevent labels from being easily smeared or washed off, avoid using felt-tip pens and cover the labels with clear plastic tape.

Packaging supplies are often sold in drug, variety, and discount stores, as well as your local post office. Some businesses not only sell postal supplies but also gift-wrap, package, and send boxes for an additional charge.

Also for a price, various delivery services can get your package anywhere, anytime. Nevertheless, it's smart to mail early anyway—not only for peace of mind, but because delivery services—

such as parcel post, United Parcel Service, and Federal Express—are swamped during the holidays and can get backed up or make a mistake.

Other couriers—including other express-mail companies, bus-line, and railway delivery—have different rates and schedules. Some will pick up packages from your home free or for a charge, others don't. Call ahead for packaging and delivery specifics, since this information can change from year to year.

Returning Gifts

Always keep receipts for your gifts and hope that others do the same. If it's questionable whether your gift will fit or please the recipient—and it's both acceptable to you and convenient for him to return it himself—send the receipt with the gift, even if it means they'll know how much you spent. If the gift was mail-ordered, include the packing slip and catalog or address, too. Although providing the receipt allows one to return the gift discreetly, you can always offer to do the honors yourself.

If you have gifts you'd like to return, keep in mind that most department stores require returns to be made within ten to fourteen days from date of purchase. The choice of offering a refund, exchange, or store credit is the option of the retailer and must be indicated clearly at the time of purchase. To save yourself time, first call the customer-service department of the store or mail-order house for requirements. In many cases, the receipt and original packaging will be necessary to make a return. (*See also Mail Ordering; Santa Claus; Saturnalia; Wise Men.*)

"Gift of the Magi"

See Poems and Stories.

Gold

According to the story of the first Christmas, three wise men came to the infant Jesus and presented him with gifts from their homelands. Melchior, King of Arabia, brought a casket of gold in the form of a shrine to signify acceptance of the child as king. Gold is one of the first known and most historically valued of all metals; gold cups and jewelry were made as early as 3,500 years before the birth of Jesus. Gold also denotes a color, the deep-yellow shade of the metal. Perhaps not coincidentally, gold is also one of the popular colors used to celebrate Christmas. (*See also The First Christmas; Myrrh; Santa Claus; Wise Men; Colors, Christmas.*)

Goodwill

The custom of extending benevolence and mercy to those less fortunate at Christmastime is an acknowledgment of the first Christmas, when angels appeared to the shepherds and said, "Glory to God in the highest, and on earth peace, good will toward men." (Luke 2) From the good-hearted who perform charitable acts all year-round to people whose consciences are roused but once a year, Christmas is the time for doing good deeds.

Tales of generosity and kindness recur throughout Christmas legend and lore. The earliest example of goodwill was furnished by the three kings, who presented precious gifts to a family in a

stable. Perhaps the best-known benefactor of the needy was St. Nicholas, or the fourth-century Bishop of Myra. This patron saint of children was known for giving his money to the poor and was the inspiration for the Santa Claus we know today.

One of the best-known of the more modern do-gooders is the Salvation Army. A world-wide Christian body with a semimilitary structure, the Salvation Army's work—which is to provide food, shelter, clothing, and religious spirit to the needy—has nothing specifically to do with Christmas. Yet a distinctive feature of the group is its holiday street-corner fund-raising: Stationed with a bell for ringing in contributions and a pot for collecting them, Army workers are a familiar seasonal sight. Founded by a Methodist minister in London in 1878, the Salvation Army is also known for providing Christmas meals and gifts for needy individuals.

Not all Christmas charities are the work of charitable organizations. Civic, school, church, and business groups have been known to raise funds for a good cause or provide gifts for a needy family. Newspapers, radio, and television stations usually use their power to elicit the goodwill of their audiences. Among the most traditional of charitable acts are parties, visits, and gifts for those in prison, the hospital, or nursing homes at Christmas.

Every year, examples of the Christmas spirit in action are endless—one only need pick up a newspaper or turn on the six o'clock news to see that. Sometimes the charitable act is quite elaborate and generous; other times it's as simple as a dime tossed into a collection bucket or a fruit basket delivered to a lonely elderly person. In any case, the Christmas spirit still seems to be alive and well. (*See also Seals, Christmas.*)

Hanukkah

Like Christmas, Hanukkah is a religious celebration including the exchange of gifts and contributions made to the poor. Hanukkah usually falls in the month of December as well. But for the most part, the similarities end there. Unlike Christmas, Hanukkah is a Jewish holiday. It begins on the eve of the twenty-fifth day of the Hebrew month of Kislev and lasts eight days. The Hebrew word Hanukkah, also written Hannuka or Chanukah, means "dedication." Also known as the Feast of Dedication or Lights, Hanukkah commemorates the rededication of the Temple of Jerusalem in 165 B.C. after its defilement by Syrian idols.

For Jews, the highlight of Hanukkah is the lighting of the menorah, an eight-arm candelabra. One candle is lit during each evening of the holiday, until eight burning candles stand together on the last night. The candles and the eight nights signify the Jews of Judea's discovery of a single jar of oil after the rededication. It was estimated that the oil would light a holy lamp for only one day, but miraculously, the lamp burned for eight days.

Holly

Holly is a beloved Christmas plant because of its bright red berries and sturdy, shiny leaves. This family of trees and shrubs was once called the "holy tree" because it was used in houses and churches at Christmastime. The word holly may have come from this name.

History

Like the other Christmas evergreens, holly's history is steeped in superstition since it continued to live when all other plants were bare and brown. Because of this unusual ability, holly was believed to have magical powers and the power to drive demons away. Germans considered holly to be a good luck charm against hostile forces of nature. In old England unmarried women were supposed to tie a sprig of holly to their beds to ward off ghosts and demons. In Louisiana the berries of the plant were valued in protecting both animals and humans from lightning, fire, and the evil eye.

According to English belief, holly even held prophetic properties. To induce a dream of his or her future mate, a young person would pick nine holly leaves in silence on a Friday at midnight, then tie them with nine knots into a three-cornered handker-

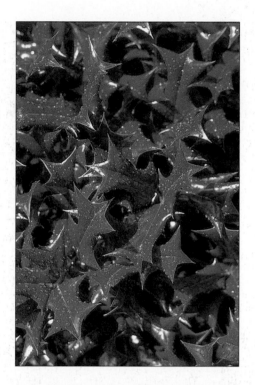

chief, which was then placed under a pillow. If the curious one remained silent from the time of the picking of the leaves until the next morning, his or her future mate was supposed to appear in a dream. In some districts the prickly-leaved holly was known as "he" and the smooth-leaved as "she," and the type that was brought into the house at Christmas was thought to indicate which sex would be ruling the roost for the coming year.

The early Church tried to stamp out the heathen custom of decorating homes, halls, and even churches with greenery, but finally gave in and attached Christian significance to these plants. Holly became associated with the Passion, the leaves representing Christ's crown of thorns and the berries the drops of blood. It was also held to be the symbol of the burning bush in which God appeared to Moses. In Denmark the holly was known as the Kristdorn, or Christ Thorn.

Holly has long been thought to be in opposition to ivy, perhaps because ivy was traditionally associated with

Bacchanalian feasts, whereas holly belonged to the realm of Church and the home. In early English carols holly stood for the man and clinging ivy for the woman in the eternal battle of the sexes.

Species

The holly tree belongs to the family *Aquifoliaceae*, and the different species—some of which are deciduous—which make up the genus *Ilex*, grow in temperate climates in most parts of the world. The native American holly tree (*Ilex opaca*) usually grows 40 to 50 feet high, though the tallest have grown to 100 feet. The dark green leaves have a leathery surface and spines along the edge. The common North American species grows in many Atlantic and Gulf states from Massachusetts to Texas and has less brilliant leaves and berries than the English holly (*I. aquifolium*), which bears white flowers in May. Yet the leaves and fruits of both are very decorative. The red fruits are not real berries, but drupes. They appear only on the pistillate, or female, trees.

Decorating with Holly

- Although a few well-placed sprigs of holly can dress up a mantel or window for Christmas, strewing it everywhere—on sconces and chandeliers around brass candlesticks, above doors, atop shelves and cupboards—imparts vital energy to the atmosphere.
- Fill a wire egg basket with holly and berries, or tie a mass of holly with a bright ribbon at the base of a grapevine wreath for the door.
- Metals—coppery brass, pewter, iron—contrast well with greens and reds, so fill a bowl, vase, or pot with crushed newspaper and top it with holly and berries. (*See also Decorations; Wreaths; Ivy.*)

THE HOLLY AND THE IVY

The holly and the ivy,
When they are both full grown,
Of all the trees that are in the wood,
The holly bears the crown.
The rising of the sun
And the running of the deer,
The playing of the merry organ,
Sweet singing in the choir.

The holly bears a blossom
As white as the lily flower,
And Mary bore sweet Jesus Christ
To be our sweet saviour.

The holly bears a berry
As red as any blood,
And Mary bore sweet Jesus Christ
To do poor sinners good.

The holly bears a prickle
As sharp as any thorn,
And Mary bore sweet Jesus Christ
On Christmas day in the morn.

The holly bears a bark
As bitter as any gall,
And Mary bore sweet Jesus Christ
For to redeem us all.

The holly and the ivy,
When they are both full grown,
Of all the trees that are in the wood
The holly bears the crown.

—Old English Carol

Home

See Family.

Hope, Bob

Although he was a comedian in motion pictures, radio, and television, Bob Hope may be the best known for entertaining United States troops during World War II, the Korean War, and the Vietnam War. His overseas Christmas shows often won the most acclaim. The first one, in Berlin in 1948, was broadcast over the radio back to the United States. In 1954 the first Hope show to be broadcast on television was filmed in Greenland.

For many years to come, Hope's Christmas shows in various parts of the world would captivate audiences back home, and in 1963, documentation of a tour to the Far East won a Golden Globe Award and was nominated for an Emmy Award. The "Last Christmas Show" in 1972 in Vietnam drew critical acclaim from columnists and editors all over the United States. According to William Robert Faith, author of *Bob Hope: A Life in Comedy*, the entertainer enjoyed his years as "the soldier in greasepaint" as much as the GIs loved to see him come: "For Hope, that sound, that din of whistles, that rise and fall of laughter…was intoxicating. When the results appeared on film; the expressions on so many close-up faces, those portraits of ecstasy, wonder and the sadness of separation from home, made the Christmas shows unique among entertainment offerings…."

International Christmases

Some of the Yuletide customs of other countries might seem unusual to North Americans, whereas others aren't all that different. When people from other countries first settled in the New World, they carried the traditions of the old countries to their new homes. Some of these traditions have faded, but today many live on.

In the United States and Canada, families traditionally gather at Christmas to visit and exchange gifts. Some families open their gifts on Christmas Day, others on Christmas Eve. The turkey and poinsettia are American innovations that have spread around the world, whereas the communal Christmas tree is America's special Yuletide trademark.

The custom of hanging stockings by

✦ the fireplace in hopes that Santa Claus will fill them with special treats came from England, except English children are more likely to know the benevolent gift-giver as Father Christmas. The British call the day after Christmas Boxing Day, when most families give money to the postman, milkman, or other persons who have served them through the year.

✦ In France children put their shoes on the doorstep on Christmas Eve so *Le Petit Noel*, the Christ Child, can fill them with gifts. They traditionally attend Midnight Mass on Christmas Eve, and then eat *le reveillon*, or late supper.

✦ People in Germany often make their own Christmas gifts. Everyone gathers on Christmas Eve for the

Bescherung, a ceremony to light the Christmas tree. Afterwards, the children usually receive their gifts. Christmas Eve is also the time to light the last candle of the Advent wreath. Many Germans enjoy roast goose for Christmas dinner.

In Switzerland folk belief has it that animals can speak at midnight on Christmas Eve.

The Christmas crib, or *presepio,* is the center of Christmas festivities in Italy. After they fast on the day before Christmas, Italians hold a ceremony around the crib—the family prays as the mother places a figure of the infant Jesus in the manger. Then the family exchanges gifts. Children receive their treats from *La Befana,* an elderly fairy queen who comes down the chimney on the Eve of Epiphany, January 6.

After Christmas Eve Midnight Mass in Spain, the streets are filled with dancers and onlookers. Spaniards actually begin their celebration on December 8, when the weeklong Feast of the Immaculate Conception begins with decorated porches and balconies and candles burning through the night.

December 25 in Belgium is a day for religion, during which the children march to church carrying crucifixes and shrines. St. Nicholas calls first to learn how children have behaved during the year, then again on December 26 with gifts for the good ones. Children in the Netherlands and Luxembourg celebrate these two dates the same way, except Holland specializes in St. Nicholas Eve parties on December 25.

In Norway the Yuletide season starts on St. Thomas's Day, December 21, when locals bake special cakes. Another Norwegian custom is *ringe in Julen,* or ringing in Christmas, when church bells throughout the country are rung at 4 P.M. on Christmas Eve.

St. Lucia's Day, December 13, opens the Christmas season in Sweden. St.

Lucia is celebrated as the Queen of Light, a fourth-century martyr who helped Sweden in a time of famine. On this day the eldest daughter, singing, wakes the rest of the family with Christmas cakes. And the people of all Scandinavian countries, Finland included, give food to birds at Christmas, since the ground is covered with snow.

Following a daylong fast and the Christmas Eve meal, Star-Man appears to give gifts to good children in Poland. The Poles also bake small wafers called *oplatki* and exchange them as other people do Christmas cards.

Among the traditional holiday customs in Russia are the singing of the carols, known as *Kolyadki,* the Advent fast, and the Christmas Eve supper. Straw is placed beneath the tablecloth to represent the straw in the manger.

In Czechoslovakia a girl tells her fortune by putting a cherry twig in water on December 4. If the twig blossoms before Christmas Eve, it means that she will marry sometime during the year.

Latin American countries (Mexico,

Brazil, Argentina, Puerto Rico, Bolivia, and others) have five special *fiestas* from the end of November until the first of February: The Feast of *Purissima* (the Immaculate Conception), on December 8; *Nochebuena* (Christmas Eve); Christmas Day; Holy Innocents' Day on December 28; and the Feast of the Three Kings on January 6. Purissima is a day for prayer. Christmas Eve revolves around the manger scene built by every family; the day culminates in a midnight mass known as Mass of the Rooster (*Mass de Gallo*)—it commemorates the tradition that a cock crowed in Bethlehem at midnight. Christmas Day is of less importance in these countries than Christmas Eve, since gifts are usually exchanged on January 6. And Holy Innocents' Day is reserved for playing practical jokes. Most countries celebrate these feasts in much the same way, with minor variations. Children in Guatemala, Honduras, and Mexico, for example, enjoy the *piñata,* a colorful figure filled with candy and gifts that is broken by a blindfolded child with a stick.

As a main dish on Christmas, many nationalities favor roasted pork or ham, including the Finnish, Norwegians, and Spanish. British and Europeans favor the plump Christmas goose, garnished with a string of sausages. Scandinavian families traditionally enjoy dried split cod, or *lutfisk*, on Christmas. Swedes may supplement this with *Juulgrot*, a pudding of rice and milk.

Argentinians still enjoy their traditional "stuffed children" *(niños envueltos)*, which is simply stuffed beefsteak. Fresh eels are time-honored Christmas fare in parts of Italy, as are baked magi cakes (small wafers), chicken, and pork. For the French *reveillon*, their late meal after Midnight Mass, they are likely to enjoy a meal of turkey or oysters, Strasbourg (liver), and black pudding.

In Asia, the people of the Philippines call their favorite holiday dish *colacion*, made by cooking fruit with root sprouts. Christians in Iran eat no meat, milk, or eggs for the first days of December. Armenians traditionally eat fried or boiled spinach on Christmas Eve in the belief that the Virgin Mary did the same the night before Jesus was born.

Desserts are among the most tantalizing of international contributions. Shortbread, a thick, buttery cookie, is of Scottish origin. The custom of baking cookies and cakes in the shapes of animals, stars, and Christmas trees was widely practiced all over Europe, particularly in Germany and Scandinavia. In fact, many classic holiday sweets are European. *Stöllen* (fruit loaf), *lebkuchen* (a cake with honey, fruit, and nuts), and *pfeffernuesse* (spiced cookies rolled in sugar) originated in Northern Europe and were made in various ways in different regions. Recipes follow for some of the most classic international desserts.

Whatever your heritage, you are sure to enjoy this collection of holiday baked goods.

The great tradition in Australia is open-air caroling. Since the weather is the opposite of that in America, Christmas is also the time for summer activities.

Christians in China call their Santa Claus *Sheng Tan Lao Ren*, which means Holy Birthday Old Man. In Japan the observance is mainly commercial and closely tied to American traditions: the bearer of gifts is Santa Claus, Western carols are sung in Japanese, Christmas trees are decorated with lights, and turkey is served at dinner. Even though the holiday is not religious for the Japanese, Christmas is widely and energetically celebrated in Japan. *Oshogatsu,*

New Year's Day, is Japan's real holiday, celebrated with a good housecleaning, kite flying, and visiting friends. *(See also Food; Santa Claus; Stockings.)*

International Foods

Some of the world's finest—and most unusual—foods are served in honor of Christmas. Many classic Christmas dishes are English in origin, including plum pudding, mincemeat pie, and the wassail bowl. Eggnog, the best known of Christmas beverages, evolved from an English drink made with ale or wine.

HUNGARIAN CHRISTMAS NUT ROLL

♦ ⋮

This old-fashioned recipe does not really require a lot of work—just time. Plan ahead since the dough requires an overnight rise in the refrigerator.

½ cup warm water
2 tablespoons yeast
1 teaspoon sugar
1 pound butter
¾ cup sugar
6 eggs
7 cups all-purpose flour
1 teaspoon salt

Filling:
¼ cup honey
1 cup sugar
6 egg whites, beaten until stiff
1 cup golden raisins
4 cups coarsely ground walnuts or pecans
1 tablespoon vanilla
1 teaspoon cinnamon

Egg wash:
1 egg beaten with 1 teaspoon water

1. Dissolve yeast and sugar in water. Let stand until bubbly, about 5 minutes. In a large mixing bowl, cream

butter and ¾ cup of sugar. Beat in eggs, one at a time. Stir in dissolved yeast, 6 cups of flour, and salt.
2. Mix by hand and knead to make soft, but not sticky, dough, adding remaining flour as needed. Shape dough into a ball, place in an oiled bowl, cover, and refrigerate overnight.
3. To make filling, combine all filling ingredients and blend well.
4. To make rolls, remove dough from refrigerator. Punch down and knead for about 5 minutes. Allow to rise at room temperature until double in bulk (this should take about 4 hours).
5. Divide dough into 4 equal balls. Roll each ball of dough into a 13- x 15-inch oblong. Spread each with one quarter of the filling. Carefully roll up, jelly roll fashion, and pinch ends closed. Place rolls on greased baking sheets, 2 per sheet. Allow to rise for 1 hour. While dough is rising, preheat oven to 350 degrees F.
6. Brush each roll with egg wash. Bake rolls 30 to 35 minutes, until golden brown. Allow to cool thoroughly before slicing.
Makes 4 15- x 4-inch rolls

♦

♦ ⋮

HUNGARIAN WALNUT COOKIES

This is a popular cookie in Hungarian households, where it is made well in advance of the holidays and stored in cookie tins.

Pastry:
3 cups flour
½ cup sugar
1 tablespoon baking powder
½ teaspoon salt
10 tablespoons butter
1 egg
¼ cup milk

Filling:
5 egg whites
½ cup sugar
1 teaspoon cinnamon
2 teaspoons vanilla
2 cups ground walnuts

Egg wash:
1 egg beaten with 1 tablespoon water

1. Prepare the pastry: Sift flour, sugar, baking powder, and salt into large mixing bowl. Cut in butter and blend until mixture resembles coarse cornmeal.
2. Stir in egg and milk and mix until dough sticks together and forms a ball. Divide dough into six balls. Wrap in wax paper and refrigerate until ready to use.
3. Prepare filling: Beat egg whites until they start to thicken. Slowly pour in sugar, beating until stiff peaks form. Stir in cinnamon, vanilla, and walnuts.
4. Preheat oven to 375 degrees F. Grease 2 to 3 cookie sheets.
5. Roll each ball of dough to about ¼-inch thick circle. Cut circle into 8 pie-like wedges. Place 1½ to 2 teaspoons of mixture at wide end of each wedge. Starting at wide end, roll up each wedge. Place cookies on cookie sheets, brush with egg wash, and bake for 10–15 minutes, just until lightly golden.
Makes 4 dozen

JULEBROD (NORWEGIAN SAFFRON BRAID)

Norway's Julebrod, or Julekake, can be baked in various fancy shapes—half moons, wreaths, figures of eight.

1 teaspoon saffron (about 20 threads)
2 tablespoons yeast
½ cup warm water
1 teaspoon sugar
¾ cup milk
½ cup sugar
1 teaspoon salt
1 stick butter at room temperature
1 beaten egg
½ cup currants
½ cup raisins
4 to 4½ cups flour
1 egg yolk beaten with 2 teaspoons water
¼ cup slivered almonds

1. Combine saffron with 1 tablespoon boiling water and set aside to soak.
2. Stir yeast into water and add 1 teaspoon sugar. Allow to stand until bubbly.
3. Heat milk until just before boiling. Stir in sugar, salt, and butter and stir until butter melts. Allow to cool to lukewarm.
4. Combine saffron, yeast mixture, and milk-butter mixture in a large mixing bowl. Stir in beaten egg, currants, and raisins. Gradually stir in 4 cups flour, mixing until dough is manageable. Add more flour as necessary. Knead dough until smooth and satiny. Place in oiled mixing bowl and set in a warm spot to rise until double in bulk—about 1 hour.
5. Punch down dough and knead for 5 minutes. Divide dough into 3 equal parts. Roll each part into a rope, about 15 inches long. On a greased baking sheet, braid the three ropes, pinching ends together tightly. Allow to rise 1 hour. While dough is rising, preheat oven to 375 degrees F.
6. Brush bread with egg-yolk glaze and sprinkle with almonds. Bake for 15 minutes, then lower oven to 350 degrees F and bake another 40 minutes, or until cake is golden brown and sounds hollow when gently rapped on the bottom.
Makes 1 loaf

OEUFS A LA NEIGE

A classic French dessert, these "floating islands" make an exquisite centerpiece dessert. They are actually snowy eggs in a vanilla-bean sauce. Serve them in a fancy crystal punch bowl.

4½ cups milk
1 vanilla bean, cut into 1-inch pieces
6 eggs, separated
1 cup superfine sugar
1 to 1½ cups cream
2 cups fresh or frozen strawberries, raspberries, or other berries (optional)
mint sprigs for garnish (optional)

1. In a 6- or 8-quart pot, heat the milk and vanilla bean just until simmering. Adjust heat as necessary to keep from boiling. Stir to keep skin from forming.
2. Meanwhile, beat the egg whites. When they begin to thicken, slowly sprinkle in ½ cup of the sugar and continue beating until fairly stiff, but not dry, peaks form.
3. Using two tablespoons, form the beaten whites into egg-shapes—

don't worry how irregular they are—and drop into the simmering milk. Do not crowd the "meringues"—allow them plenty of space. They will souffle to double in size at first. Cook them gently for 2 to 3 minutes on each side, turning only once. Use a slotted spoon to turn very gently. The meringues will shrink back to size when turned. As they are finished, place them on paper towels to drain and cool. Reserve the cooking milk.

You can make the meringues up to two days in advance and store them in a tightly covered bowl or container between layers of paper towel.

4. To make the custard, strain 1 cup of the reserved milk and combine with the cream and remaining sugar in a heavy-bottom 2-quart saucepan. Cook over low heat until sugar is dissolved.

5. Beat the egg yolks in a bowl, then slowly beat in about ½ cup of the hot milk mixture. Slowly stir the egg mixture back into the saucepan. Cook custard over low to medium heat, stirring constantly, until thickened, about 15 minutes. Cool to room temperature. (You can make custard up to 2 days in advance. Store, covered, in refrigerator.)

6. To serve, have custard and meringue islands chilled or at room temperature. Pour the custard into a decorative glass bowl. Gently set the meringues in, spooning custard sauce over them. Top with sliced strawberries or whole berries. Serve each person 2 islands with some sauce and berries.

For an extra festive garnish, top the islands with sprigs of fresh mint leaves, if available.

Serves 10 to 12

PECAN BISCOTTI

The traditional biscotti use filberts (hazelnuts) and are dry, hard cookies great for dunking. This recipe yields a more buttery cookie that is semihard and a little chewier. It's good to keep on hand to serve with wine or coffee to drop-in company.

2 cups pecan halves, roasted
12 tablespoons butter (1½ sticks) at
    room temperature
¾ cups sugar
2 eggs
2 cups whole wheat pastry flour
1 tablespoon baking powder
½ teaspoon salt

1. Preheat oven to 350 degrees F. Grease 2 cookie sheets. Chop 1 cup of the pecans.

2. Beat butter and sugar in a large bowl. Beat in eggs, one at a time.

3. Sift together chopped nuts, flour, baking powder, and salt. Add gradually to batter, blending only until evenly mixed. Stir in remaining whole nuts. Dough will be soft.

4. Divide dough into quarters. Oiling hands if dough is too sticky, shape each quarter into a 12-inch long strip, 2 to 2½ inches wide on the cookie sheet. Place 2 strips on each cookie sheet.

5. Bake for 15 minutes, or until light golden brown. Remove from oven, cut diagonally into ½-inch thick slices. Carefully turn each slice on its side, and bake for another 7 minutes, or until slightly toasted.

6. Remove slices to a wire rack and allow to cool completely. Cookies keep well for 2 months if wrapped and stored in a tightly sealed container in a cool spot.
Makes 4 dozen

PFEFFERNUESSE (PEPPER NUTS)

In Denmark they're called *pebernodder*, in Sweden, *pepparnotter*. Northern Europeans wouldn't be without them during the Yuletide. This version is not as rock hard and crunchy as the traditional pfeffernuesse, but chewy, dense, and very fragrant with spices and liquor.

½ cup butter
½ cup brown sugar
2 eggs
1 teaspoon orange or lemon zest
⅔ cup ground almonds
⅓ cup brandy or rum
¼ cup molasses
2 cups flour
1 teaspoon baking powder
1 teaspoon cinnamon
1 teaspoon cloves
½ teaspoon ground anise or cardamom
½ teaspoon black pepper

1. Preheat oven to 350 degrees F. Grease several cookie sheets.
2. Cream butter and sugar. Beat in eggs, one at a time.
3. Add zest, almonds, liquor, and molasses and mix well.
4. Combine remaining dry ingredients in a separate bowl. Fold into wet ingredients just until blended.
5. Shape dough into 1-inch balls and place on cookie sheets. Bake 7 to 10 minutes, until lightly browned on bottom. Cookies may still be soft when first removed from oven, but will firm up as they cool. If you prefer a harder cookie, bake a little longer.
Makes 4 to 5 dozen

PIZZELLE

You can find a waffle iron made especially for making pizzelle in Italian markets; or you can use a regular waffle iron if the iron has a shallow side to it (generally reversible). These fancy, textured cookies make a nice gift, either alone or as part of a mixed cookie tray.

6 eggs, beaten
3¼ cups sugar
2 sticks unsalted butter, melted
2 teaspoons vanilla
3½ cups flour
1 tablespoon baking powder
½ teaspoon salt
1 teaspoon ground fennel *or* ½ teaspoon anise flavoring

1. Heat pizzelle or waffle iron. Beat eggs and sugar together until evenly mixed. Stir in cooled butter and vanilla.
2. Sift together flour, baking powder, salt, and ground fennel or anise. Stir dry ingredients into egg mixture and blend well. Dough will be sticky.
3. Drop by tablespoonfuls (1 tablespoon per cookie) onto prepared waffle iron. Cool and sprinkle with powdered sugar.
Makes about 4 dozen

SCANDINAVIAN GINGERSNAPS

4 tablespoons sugar
1/2 cup molasses
2 tablespoons vegetable oil
2 tablespoons milk
2 1/4 cups flour
1/2 teaspoon baking soda
1/2 teaspoon salt
1 teaspoon cinnamon
1/2 teaspoon ginger
powdered sugar (optional)

1. Mix sugar with liquids and stir well. Reserve 1/4 cup of flour and sift together remaining dry ingredients.
2. Add sifted ingredients to liquids, one fourth at a time, while mixing well. Work the dough with your hands until it is smooth. If it seems too soft, add little more of the flour; if it is too crumbly, add a few more drops of milk. Wrap dough in plastic and chill for 2 hours or overnight.
3. Preheat oven to 350°F. Grease cookie sheets. Roll out the dough to 1/4-inch thickness. Use cookie cutters to stamp out various shapes. Or use an overturned glass with a 3-inch diameter to press out circles of dough. Bake cookies for 10 minutes, until lightly browned. If you wish, sprinkle with powdered sugar when cooled.

STRUFOLI

These honey-sweet, chewy bits of deep-fried egg dough are commonly seen around Italian homes at Christmastime. They're eaten as snacks or served on a tray with other Christmas cookies.

2½ cups all-purpose flour
½ teaspoon salt
2 eggs
1 egg yolk
3 cups vegetable oil
¾ cup honey
¼ cup sugar
1 tablespoon colored sprinkles
   (optional)
¼ cup chopped candied fruit
   (optional)

1. Combine flour and salt. With a fork, slowly stir in eggs and egg yolk, mixing to make a soft dough. Knead until smooth, adding a little more flour if necessary.

2. Heat oil in a deep fryer (to 375 degrees F) or in a large, heavy-bottom skillet. Break off pieces of the dough, about the size of marbles. Drop them into the hot oil, not over-crowding, and stir gently. Dough bits will brown in about 1 to 2 minutes. Remove them with a slotted spoon and drain on absorbent paper. Continue until all dough is used up. When they are thoroughly cooled and drained, place all the fried dough bits in a large bowl.

3. Heat honey and sugar in a saucepan until sugar is dissolved, about 5 minutes. Distribute hot honey evenly over dough bits, tossing gently. Add sprinkles and candied fruit if desired. These keep well up to 2 months if wrapped tightly and refrigerated.
Makes about 4 cups

✦ Ivy

Any one of a large number of creeping or climbing ornamental vines is known as ivy, but at Christmastime we typically see sprigs of English, or common, ivy (*Hedera helix*). The plant is a member of the ginseng family, Araliaceae, and its waxy leaves have five points, or angles. It can cling to smooth surfaces with the fine aerial roots on its stems. Evergreens are traditional decorations at Christmas because they remain lush and green even during the cold dark month of December.

Like holly and the other evergreens, ivy has been associated with superstition for ages. For example, ivy was thought to foretell the future. In Scotland, a young woman curious about her future spouse could hold an ivy leaf to her heart and recite: "Ivy, Ivy, I love you;/In my bosom I put you,/The first young man who speaks to me/My future husband shall be."

Unlike holly, however, ivy was long banished from use in Christian homes and churches, since it was the ancient symbol of Bacchus, the god of wine and revelry. Ivy's frequent association with holly was not favorable, either—in early English carols holly stood for resiliency and manhood whereas ivy was female and clinging. (*See also Decorations; Holly; Wreath.*)

✦ Lights, Christmas

The use of decorative lights at Christmas symbolizes Christ as the Light of the World. For a thousand years Europeans lit candles in their churches and homes on Christmas Eve to welcome the Christ child. Today, the candle is still a favorite Yuletide decoration and is used on mantels, in windows, as centerpieces, and during church ceremonies.

Martin Luther, the leader of the Protestant Reformation in sixteenth-century Germany, was thought to be the first person to put lighted tapers on his Christmas tree to represent the stars above Bethlehem on the night of Christ's birth. Soon others followed his example, but the problem of attaching the candles and the danger of fire
✦ prompted the invention of electric

Christmas lights in 1882, just three years after Thomas Edison invented the lightbulb.

As electric tree lights were perfected, they became less expensive and more common. They also took on many shapes and forms. In the early days, for example, tree bulbs were miniature versions of the household light of the day. In about 1910 the bulbs took on color and a ball shape. By 1919 animal, star, and Santa Claus shapes were produced. In the twenties, Viennese-painted birds, flowers, and fruits that lit up were popular. Conventional Christmas trees often feature flashing lights and miniature lights, which were first developed in the thirties. The forties and fifties saw the introduction of novelty liquid-filled bubble lights.

Electric lights are in no way limited to the decoration of Christmas trees—

they're also used to festoon windows; doors; railings; angels, Santa Clauses, and other outdoor figurines; and even the outlines of houses and buildings themselves. Many cities and communities in the United States hold lighting contests and give prizes to the homes or businesses that are most thoughtfully or elaborately decorated.

Electric Light Safety

Every year, inspect your lights before using them. Each string of lights should carry the official Underwriters' Laboratories (UL) label. Check for cracked insulation and bare or broken wires, especially where wires enter the socket. Discard damaged or worn-out strings. If a strand appears safe, plug it into a wall socket for fifteen minutes and check for signs of smoking or melting.

Outdoors, use only weatherproof

lights and wires. If you use an extension cord, wrap the junction of the light plug and extension cord with electrical tape.

Also avoid overloading electrical circuits. If you have a number of strings of lights, plug them into different sockets. Never connect more than two hundred midget lights or more than fifty large lamps through miniature lamp sets.

Avoid leaving lights on when away from home or asleep. Use only a fresh tree and stand it in water so it doesn't dry out. Try to hang lamps so they're not in actual contact with the green of the tree or ornaments. It's best to let lights burn for only a short time, too. Remember that when hot bulbs come in contact with a dried-out tree, a fire can start—and a tree can be completely consumed in flames within seconds. (*See also Candles; Tree, Christmas; Decorating.*)

m

Mail, Christmas

See Cards, Christmas; Gifts.

Mail Order

When the first mail-order firm, Montgomery Ward and Company, was established in 1862, most of their customers lived on farms and in small towns. Modern catalogs reflect the fact that city people as well as country people buy from these books.

In fact, the mail-order business has recently seen a surge of interest from Americans, who not only have less time to shop, but are drawn in by the expanded, diversified selection. There are catalogs for art-lovers (The Metropolitan Museum of Art), cooks (Williams-Sonoma), fishermen (L.L.

Bean), and needlepointers (The Stitchery). Baklava (Harry and David), baby clothes (Hanna), and burritos (Burrito Express) may be delivered right to your door, and so can a new pair of boxer shorts (Brooks Brothers), field boots (Eddie Bauer), or bikini underwear (Victoria's Secret).

For many, ordering from catalogs is the ideal way to Christmas shop. Knowing this, retailers roll out extra shipments of special Christmas catalogs. Remember to allow enough time for a mail-order gift to arrive for Christmas—some firms, like L.L. Bean, are swift, but delivery companies like United Parcel Service are extra-busy during the holidays. Most mail-order houses offer express delivery for an extra charge. Ask about these details.

Here are some addresses and telephone numbers of prominent mail-order firms. For a more exhaustive list, write to the Direct Marketing Association, 11 West 42nd Street, New York, NY 10036, for its Great Catalog Guide, $3.

L.L. Bean, Inc.
Freeport, ME 04033-0001
(800) 221-4221

The Metropolitan Museum of Art
Special Service Office
Middle Village, NY 11381-0001
(800) 635-5355

✦ J. Crew
One Ivy Crescent
Lynchburg, VA 24506-1001
(800) 562-0258

Burrito Express
Pasadena, CA 91104
(800) 553-8388

Harry and David
Medford, OR 97501-0712
(503) 776-2400

Hanna Anderson
1010 N.W. Flanders Street
Portland, OR 97209
(800) 222-0544

Victoria's Secret
P.O. Box 16589
Columbus, OH 43216-6589
✦ (800) 888-1500

✦ Eddie Bauer
P.O. Box 3700
Seattle, WA 98124-3700
(800) 426-8020

Williams-Sonoma
P.O. Box 7456
San Francisco, CA 94120-7456
(415) 421-4242

Brooks Brothers
350 Campus Plaza
P.O. Box 4016
Edison, NJ 08818-4016
(800) 274-1815

Tiffany & Co.
P.O. Box 5477
Parsippany, NJ 07054-9957
(800) 526-0649

Coach
300 Chubb Avenue
Lyndhurst, NJ 07071-3577
(800) 223-8647

Spiegel
Suite A
1040 W. 35th Street
Chicago, IL 60672-0040
(800) 345-4500

Manger

See Nativity Scenes.

Mary

✦ *See The First Christmas.*

Mistletoe

One of the most popular and legendary of the Christmas greens, mistletoe is an evergreen that belongs to *Loranthaceae*, the laurel family. It has yellow twigs, poisonous waxy white berries, and thickly clustered light-green leaves. A parasite, it grows most often on the trunks and branches of apple, lime, hawthorn, sycamore, poplar, locusts, fir, and occasionally on oak trees. Mistletoe species grow both in America and Europe. True mistletoe, *Viscumalbum*, has short and round leaves, compared to the American type, *Phoradendron flavescens*, whose leaves have a longer and more graceful shape.

There are several explanations for the mistletoe's name. The dictionary attributes its origin to the Anglo-Saxon "mistel" plus "tan," which means "differ-

In ancient times, mistletoe was regarded as a symbol of future hope and peace. Whenever enemies met under the plant they dropped their weapons and embraced. The current custom of kissing under the mistletoe may have grown out of this age-old practice.

ent twig," probably because the plant forms such a strong contrast to the tree on which it grows. The word might come from the missel thrush, a bird that feeds on waxlike white mistletoe berries and therefore contributes to the plant's wide distribution.

Actually, it was the Druids, the

ancient priests of the Celts, who insisted that mistletoe had been brought from heaven by the missel thrush. Consequently, they used the plant in their sacrifices to the gods. The Celtics also believed that mistletoe had miraculous healing powers—the name for the plant in the Celtic languages is "all-heal."

There are many other legends associated with the mistletoe as well. In Greek mythology, the evergreen was believed to be a charm to ward off evil; in the tale of Aeneas, a "golden bough" guided him through the underworld to see his father and back to earth again.

In Northern mythology, an arrow made of mistletoe killed Balder, the sun god and son of Frigga. Through the power of Frigga's love, Balder returned to life and Frigga's tears turned into mistletoe berries, symbolic of love that

*"When blushing lips, that
   smile at folly,
As red as berries on the holly,
Kiss, and banish melancholy.
Oh, oh, the mistletoe!"*
—*song from the mid-1800s,
author unknown*

is stronger than death. Overjoyed by her son's return to life, Frigga kissed each person who passed beneath the mistletoe. Scandinavians and Romans considered the plant to be a symbol of hope and peace: When enemies from either nationality met under it, they laid aside their weapons, kissed each other, and declared a truce until the next day.

The pleasant symbolism of mistletoe may account for the fact that in many countries, a person caught standing beneath mistletoe, usually hung over a doorway, must forfeit a kiss. It is not known, though, how kissing under the mistletoe became a Christmas custom. In fact, some early Christians associated the plant with evil because of its connection with pagan Druid rites.

In any case, the mistletoe has long been a symbol of holiday mirth and superstition, particularly in England, where until recently it was considered unlucky for a home *not* to have a sprig of its own. In fact, eighteenth-century England is credited with a special kissing ball made with mistletoe, beneath which partygoers would play kissing games. Here is one such game:

Hang the mistletoe from the ceiling, then form a circle around it. The first player slides a shoe toward the mistletoe, but if he fails to land it directly beneath the suspended plant, another player tries. The first player to land the shoe under the mistletoe must kiss the closest male or female toward which the shoe points. (*See also Evergreens.*)

Moore, Clement C.

See "A Visit from St. Nicholas."

Movies

From the first adaptation of Charles Dickens's *A Christmas Carol* to the madcap modern *Ernest Saves Christmas*, movies with a holiday plot are plentiful. Some of them, like Frank Capra's *It's a Wonderful Life*, are classics. Others, like 1987's *Christmas Comes to Willow Creek*, a spin-off of the television show *Dukes of Hazzard*, are less memorable. But nearly all resurface on television every holiday season.

Christmas wouldn't be Christmas, for instance, without at least one reshowing of *A Christmas Carol*. The first one, directed by Edwin L. Martin, starred Reginald Owen as Scrooge and gave young June Lockhart her screen debut. The 1951 British version starring Alastair Sims is the best remem-

bered and most critically acclaimed. More recent interpretations by George C. Scott and Albert Finney have also won recognition. *An American Christmas Carol* (1979) sets the Dickensian tale in America, with Henry Winkler in the principal role.

It's a Wonderful Life, the 1946 film starring Jimmy Stewart and Donna Reed, tells the story of George Bailey, a man living in a small town running a small savings and loan. When he questions the worthiness of his life one snowy Christmas Eve, an angel appears to save him and boost his Christmas spirit. The movie was based on a short story, "The Greatest Gift," by Philip Van Doren Stern. In 1977 Marlo Thomas starred in a television remake, *It Happened One Christmas*. In 1985 the Ted Turner-owned MGM-UA Entertainment Corporation

acquired the rights to the original and computer-colorized it.

Another Christmas classic, *Miracle on 34th Street*, has also been computer-colorized and remade for television. The 1947 original starred Oscar-winner Edmund Gwenn as Kris Kringle, who works in Macy's and has to go on trial to prove he's Santa Claus, and Natalie Wood. The 1973 version featured Sebastian Cabot (as Santa, of course), Jane Alexander, David Hartman, Jim Backus, Tom Bosley, and Suzanne Davidson.

Another old-time favorite is *Christmas in Connecticut* (1945), starring Barbara Stanwyck. It is about a magazine columnist without homemaking skills who must entertain her boss and a war

Lead actor Jimmy Stewart and director Frank Capra received Academy Award nominations for their work in the 1946 movie It's a Wonderful Life. *Also nominated for the year's best picture award, the film is arguably Capra's best and most typical work, according to the critics.*

veteran for the holidays. *White Christmas* (1954) is a partial remake of *Holiday Inn* (1942) and features Bing Crosby's immortal crooning of the title song and Danny Kaye's dancing shenanigans.

There are several more recent films that have earned a regular place on the holiday TV schedule. *A Christmas to Remember* (1978) tells the story of an elderly farm couple who take in their city-bred grandson for the holidays—the cast includes Jason Robards, Eva Marie Saint, and Joanne Woodward. *Christmas Lilies of the Field* (1979) is a follow-up to director Ralph Nelson's Oscar-winning *Lilies of the Field* (1965). The plot concerns Homer Smith—played this time not by Sidney Poitier but by Billy Dee Williams—who returns to the Arizona chapel he built and adds an orphanage and kindergarten to the site.

Among the 1980's movies vying for a permanent position on the Christmas viewing roster is the made-for-TV *Christmas Eve* (1986), in which Loretta Young stars as a millionaire who brings her grown-up grandchildren home for the holidays. Jason Robards and Julie Harris appear in the made-for-cable film *A Christmas Wife* (1988) about a lonely widower who hires a woman to be his Christmas vacation companion.

The late 1980s contributed a new roster of films with a holiday theme to the big screen. *Santa Claus: The Movie* (1985) stars Dudley Moore and John Lithgow in a tale of how Santa came to be. *Ernest Saves Christmas* (1988) features Jim Varney as the character popularized by television commercials who helps Santa get his act together. And Bill Murray stars in yet another reinterpretation of *A Christmas Carol*— *Scrooged* (1988), a comedy about a ruthless television executive who gets his comeuppances. (*See also* Dickens, Charles; Television; White Christmas.)

The 1954 film **White Christmas** *is considered by the critics to be a humdrum revamp of 1942's Holiday Inn. In* **White Christmas,** *two entertainers (Bing Crosby, Danny Kaye) boost the popularity of a winter resort run by an old army buddy.*

Music

The first melodies sung at Christmas time were the litanies, or musical prayers, of the Christian church. According to an account written by an early historian, the bishop of Rome urged his people to sing "in celebration of the birthday of our Lord" in the second century. Christmas hymns, written mostly in Latin, originated in the fifth century. The hymns were not sung by the congregation, but by the priests who strolled around their parishes on Christmas Eve.

Carols were first composed in the 1200s, when actors sang along to the Bible stories they dramatized for the church congregations. These songs weren't specifically about Christmas, but they often centered on Mary, Jesus, and the shepherds. Although the definition for "carol" was originally a French song and dance, the word eventually became associated with Christmas.

Some of the world's finest music was written for Christmas in the 1700s as well. Johann Sebastian Bach's "Christmas Oratorio" follows the Biblical text of Matthew and Luke. George Frideric Handel first presented his "Messiah" in Dublin in 1742. Louis-Hector Berlioz' dramatic cantata "The Childhood of Christ" and Peter Ilich Tchaikovsky's ballet "The Nutcracker" are other well-known classics.

More recently composed Christmas music includes "Winter Wonderland" and "Let It Snow! Let It Snow! Let It Snow!," both Tin Pan Alley creations. Both are popular songs that reflect the traditional longing for snow, though neither of these enjoyed the monu- mental success of "I'm Dreaming of a White Christmas."

This Irving Berlin composition, which was heard first in the 1942 movie *Holiday Inn*, is the all-time champ of the modern era, selling in excess of 100 million copies. Bing Crosby's time-honored release alone accounts for some 30 million sales.

Since "White Christmas," seasonal hits have come mainly from the early part of the rock era, 1955–65. The novelty record "The Chipmunk Song," from the Top 40 album "Christmas With the Chipmunks," numbers among them, as well as Nat King Cole's "The Christmas Song" and Elvis Presley's "Blue Christmas." Presley, of course, was king of Christmas music, with Top 40 albums (Elvis' Christmas Album"), and "Elvis Sings the Wonderful World of Christmas," to his credit. "Jingle Bell Rock," "Silver Bells," "The Little Drummer Boy," "Please Come Home for Christmas," and "Rockin' Around the Christmas Tree," were other extremely popular Presley tunes.

The most popular new release of the seventies was the barked version of "Jingle Bells," by the Singing Dogs. "Grandma Got Run Over by a Reindeer," a humorous hit by Elmo and Patsy, contrasted sharply with its eighties competitor, the philanthropic "Do They Know It's Christmas?" by Band Aid.

Other artists whose singles are replayed on the radio every holiday season include The Beach Boys ("Little Saint Nick"), Jose Feliciano ("Feliz Navidad"), and Merle Haggard ("If We Make It Through December"). Compilations of various artists— including "A Motown Christmas" with the Temptations, Stevie Wonder, and the Supremes, and "The Christmas Album" with Barbra Streisand,

Frank Sinatra, and Johnny Cash— have also enjoyed considerable success.

In other categories are albums by duos ("Once Upon a Christmas," Kenny Rogers and Dolly Parton), families ("The Sinatra Family Wish You a Merry Christmas"), and orchestras ("A Christmas Festival," Boston Pops Orchestra). More recent holiday albums have been recorded by Randy Travis, Wynton Marsalis, Roger Whitaker, Amy Grant, and New Kids on the Block. (*See also Carols, Christmas; White Christmas.*)

Myrrh

According to the story of the first Christmas, three Wise Men came to the infant Jesus and presented him with gifts from their homelands. Caspar, King of Taurus, brought myrrh, a fragrant gum resin used in making perfume and incense, in a gold-mounted horn to prophesize Christ's death. Myrrh comes from the resin of certain small trees of the genus *Commiphora*, which grow in eastern Africa and southern Arabia. (*See also Carols; The First Christmas; Frankincense; Gold; Wise Men.*)

Nativity Scenes

The word *nativity* refers to the circumstances or process of being born, and a nativity scene represents or reenacts the birthday story of Jesus himself.

St. Francis of Assisi, an Italian friar who lived in the early 1200s, is credited with popularizing the nativity scene. Because church services were usually conducted in Latin and the scriptures therefore could not be understood by many of his followers, St. Francis sought to humanize the Christmas story by staging a simple manger scene at Greccio, Italy, in 1224. The attendants were so impressed by the novel ceremony they repeated it year after year.

Soon the idea was adopted by other Italian towns and gradually spread to Spain, Portugal, France, England, and

to other parts of the world. The cribs became larger, more elaborate, and realistic, and whole villages and towns were constructed to reenact the Nativity. In Belgium, men, women, and children, sheep, and lambs present living tableaux of the manger scene. In Hungary, children dressed as angels or shepherds carry a crib from house to house, acting scenes from the Bible story.

Using real people and animals to stage the scene has become a popular Christmas custom for churches all over

North America as well. It is also common to see crib scenes in front of or within churches, in people's yards, and on Christmas cards.

Historically the crib was intended for public display, but during this century it has also become a domestic institution. Often the figures of the holy family, the Wise Men, shepherds, angels, and animals are family treasures, carefully wrapped and stored from year to year. These scenes are collectively known as crèches. (*See also The First Christmas; International Christmases.*)

**Christmas inspires art. Nativity
scenes (above) are a very popular subject in paintings.
Nutcracker Suite (right) is the
joining of a beautiful story,
music, and dance.**

◆ *"Nutcracker Suite"*

Composed by Peter Ilich Tchaikovsky in
1891, *Nutcracker Suite* is based on a story
by E.T.A. Hoffman, in a French
adaptation by Duman. The story tells of
a girl who receives an ugly nutcracker
for Christmas. The other children make
fun of her gift, but she lovingly defends
it and then dreams that her nutcracker
is a handsome prince. The prince leads a
victorious battle against a gang of mice,
then conducts the girl to Jam Mountain,
where there is singing, dancing, and festivities.

Tchaikovsky originally wrote this
music as a ballet, but it is the orchestral
suite that is most famous. The suite is in
eight parts: Miniature Overture; Russian
Dance; March; Dance of the Sugarplum
Fairy; Arabian Dance; Chinese Dance;
Reed-Pipe Dance; and Waltz of the
Flowers. At Christmastime "Nutcracker
Suite" is performed before audiences all
over the world. (*See also Music,
Christmas.*)

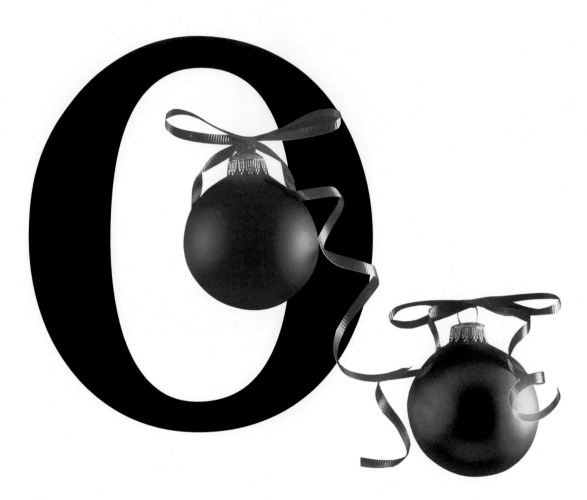

Ornaments

Before Christmas trees were dressed with manufactured decorations, fruits, candy, cookies, nuts, colored paper, small toys, pine cones, seed pods, and strings of popcorn and berries were typically used as ornaments. Most of the edible decorations—spices, butter, gingerbread cookies a half-inch thick, fruit-shaped marzipan, balls of caramelized popcorn, and paper cornucopias filled with nuts—were eaten by children when the tree was dismantled. The homemade ornaments that didn't come from the kitchen—clothespin dolls dressed in scrap fabrics; straw soaked in water and bent into star shapes, angels, and bells; and ribbon ends to make into tiny flags—were often saved for the following year.

Like the Christmas tree itself, the

custom of decorating the tree, and the mouth-watering decorations described above, commercial ornaments were originally products of Germany. The oldest were made of tin by the same mid-to-late nineteenth-century German toy makers who cast doll furniture and doll's dishes. Made in geometric shapes such as stars, crosses, and flowers, these tin ornaments usually hung from threads and were light enough to turn slowly in the air currents of the burning candles that were also popular in Germany at this time. Wax figurines of baby Jesus, angels, animals, and children and glass ornaments shaped as balls, fruits, and icicles were also among the first commercial decorations.

During the first years of the twentieth century, most North American Christmas trees were still decorated

with homemade ornaments. As more and more Germans immigrated to the United States, however, commercial ornaments quickly became available there. By the turn of the century, the choice of Christmas ornaments was staggering, from the thin strips of silver foil designed to drip from boughs like icicles to the big wax angel for the top of the tree. Yet Americans did not buy these decorations in boxes of a dozen as they would sixty years later, but one or two at a time—big ornaments in prosperous years and small ones, if any at all, in poor years. The rest of the trimmings were still homemade, and the women's magazines regularly featured do-it-yourself directions for making them, just as they do today.

But as the market for commercial ornaments spread to other nationalities than Germans, American

Old-fashioned Christmas ornaments are fragile, but cherished. The best Christmas trees mingle old and new to tell the story of a family.

Christmas trees were more and more likely to be trimmed with fancy, store-bought decorations. In 1918 the first American-produced ornaments—simple round balls made by toy manufacturers—appeared in stores. Little wagons, baby carriages, and drums domestically made from cardboard appeared during the Depression. Ultimately, the German art of glass-blowing ornaments was all but replaced when Corning perfected its machine-blown and lacquered ornaments about 1940.

Today's decorations include these brightly colored glass balls as well as ornaments made from cloth, yarn, gold-plated metals, ceramics, plastic, wood—almost every material imaginable. Since the electric light bulb was invented in 1879, of course, electric Christmas lights—a unique American contribution to the art of tree-trimming—have enjoyed a tremendous popularity.

Yet the most cherished ornaments on any modern-day Christmas tree, it seems, are not the fragile, polished, recently bought glass ornament from the most expensive department stores or the state-of-the-art string of lights, but the bottle cap, hand-decorated by a third-grader or the Santa Claus-shaped bulb from great-grandmother's Christmas tree. The more you personalize the holiday season, the more meaningful and enjoyable it will be. (*See also Decorations; Lights; Trees, Christmas.*)

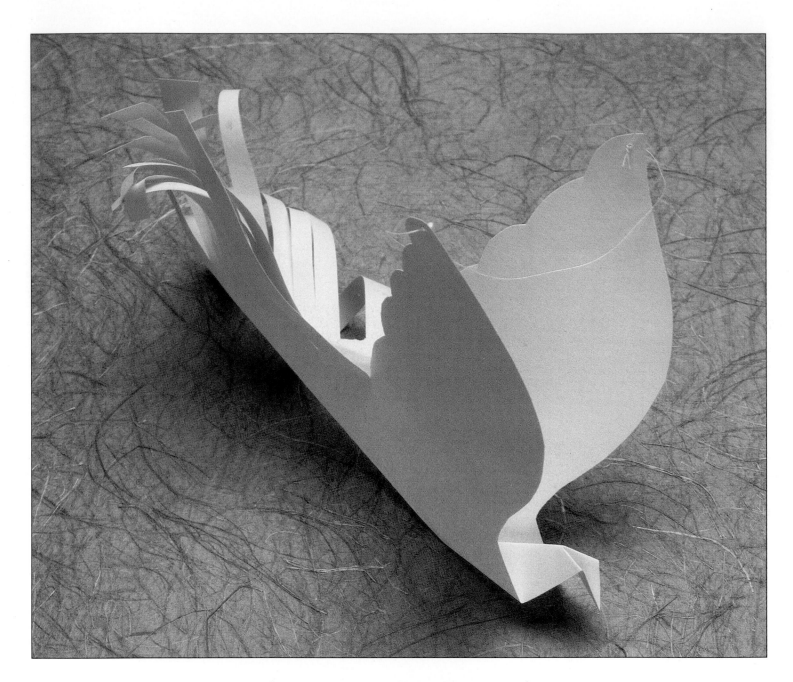

✦

PEACE ON EARTH
DOVE ORNAMENT
· · · · · · · · · ·

This ornament is surprisingly simple
to make, but it looks wonderful on a
Christmas tree, or hanging from a
doorway.

Materials:
1 piece of stiff white paper, at least
    10" x 10"
scissors
needle and white thread

✦

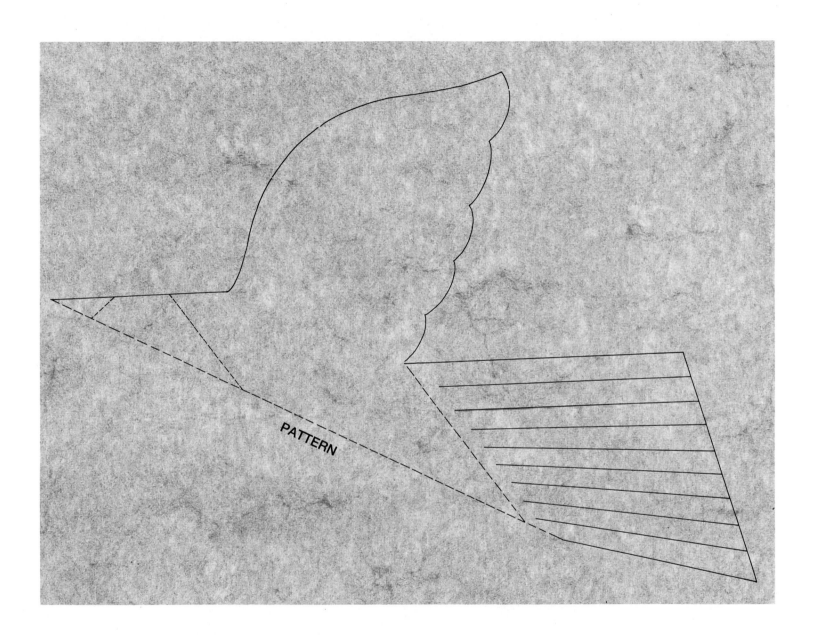

PATTERN

Directions:

1. Fold paper in half.
2. Draw the shape of a bird with a large tail on the folded paper (see illustration) and cut it out.
3. Fold each side of the tail down, as shown.
4. Make folds on either half of the bird so that the neck will fold inwards, as shown.

5. Make folds on either half of the bird's head so that it will fold down, as shown.
6. Cut streamers in the tail, that are slightly wider at the edge of the tail than at the body of the bird. Curl the edges by holding the paper between your thumb and the edge of a scissor blade, and running the blade lightly along the paper.

7. Thread the needle. Knot one end of thread and pierce the wing tip from the back, and pull the thread through so that the knot holds the thread in place. Leaving five inches of slack, pierce the other wingtip from the underside, and knot the backside of the wing. Hang the bird by this thread.

◆ STOCKING, TEDDY BEAR, AND CANDY CANE ORNAMENTS

These delightful fabric ornaments require some sewing skill to assemble. They are a pretty alternative to ball ornaments and add a homespun touch to the Christmas tree. If you are especially creative, you may think of variations on these crafts, such as Santa faces, angels, and wreaths. These could be decorated with spangles, satin ribbons, lace, and other unusual touches.

Materials:

fabric marker (or chalk, pencil, or tailor's transfer paper) for pattern

$\frac{1}{3}$ yard, 36-inch-wide unbleached muslin will make four or more ornaments

$\frac{1}{3}$ yard, 44-inch-wide red or green cotton print fabric will make backs for six ornaments

green and red embroidery floss

about 1 cup polyester filling per ornament

8 inches of $\frac{1}{4}$-inch-wide matching ribbon or ricrac for hanger

pencil, scissors, embroidery hoop, pins, thread, embroidery needle, hand sewing needle and (optionally) sewing machine ◆

1. Trace or transfer your choice of pattern to the muslin, including both the cutting line (A) and the seam lines (B). You can also transfer the embroidery pattern at this time, or mark it on free-hand. Do not cut until you are finished with the embroidery.

2. Clamp muslin into embroidery hoop and, using all six strands of the embroidery floss, embroider French knots onto the muslin, following colors indicated in pattern. Use three strands, and outline stitch for the bear's smile, and three strands and satin stitch for his bow. (See instructional drawings for stitch information.)

3. Pin muslin to cotton print fabric, right sides facing. Place carefully to conserve fabric if you intend to make many. Cut out on cutting line.

4. Place right sides together, pin, and pin the ribbon into a loop *inside* the two layers, with the tails sticking out. Sew muslin and cotton print together on seam line, catching tails of the loop in the seam and taking care not to catch it anywhere else in the seam. Leave about a ½ inch at the side. Trim corners, clip curves, and turn ornament right side out. Fill lightly with polyester filling. Stitch the small opening closed with invisible stitches.

French knot, using all 6 strands. Wrap embroidery cotton close to fabric once or more around needle. Push through same hole from which the needle emerged. Pull up firmly.

Outline stitch, using 3 strands. Backstitch, overlapping each preceding stitch by half its length.

Satin stitch. Using 3 strands, stitch over and over in stitches no more than ½ inch long, making each stitch lie exactly abutting the preceding one. This stitch is used to completely cover areas of embroidery. If you must cover an area larger than ½ inch wide, make the stitches of irregular length and overlap the next row slightly.

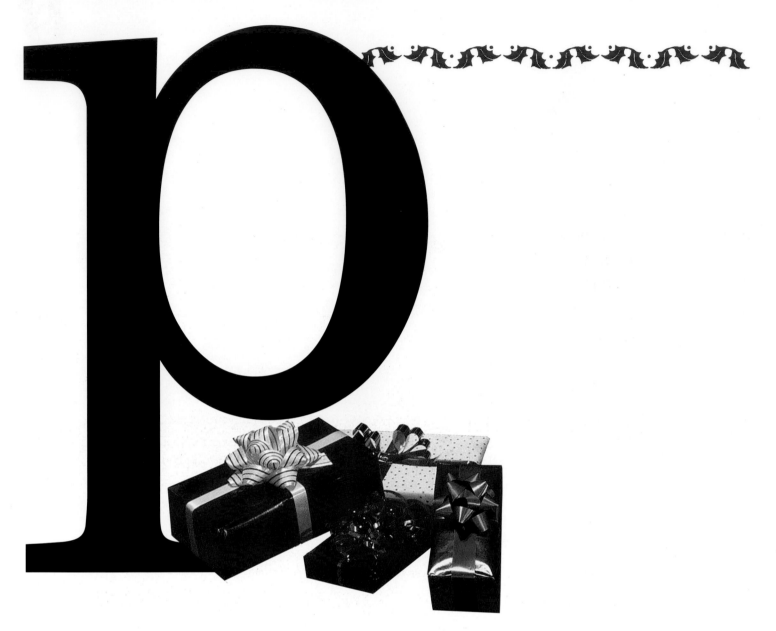

Packages *See Gifts.*

Parties, Christmas

From the perfunctory office event to the traditional family gathering, Christmas is the time for parties. Nearly every American attends at least one party during the Christmas season, whether it is a church, school, business, or neighborhood function.

At many holiday parties, gifts are exchanged. Family members and friends might select a gift for each and every person, but a very large, less intimate group might decide to "draw names" for a Christmas party. At office and business parties gifts aren't usually given.

Attending a party is one thing; giving one is another. If you plan to throw your own bash, here's what to consider:

Budget and Guest List
Think about your budget and the size of the party location. Stay within your means. Don't invite more people than you can accommodate, and try to schedule the party at a convenient time for everyone.

Type of Party
Most party-givers tend to stick with the traditional ones described above, but anything is possible. Consider a breakfast or brunch party; they're ideal when so many schedules are already occupied with evening events, and set the stage for a different kind of menu. Tree-trimming parties, when guests are invited to bring one ornament to hang on a tree, are always fun and unusual. A twist on this idea is to have guests prepare a special tree for birds and squirrels of the neighborhood, ornamented with strings of

popcorn and cranberries, small squares of suet tied in ribbon, and decorative crackers. Also consider other themes, such as a White Christmas party. Rent the movie of the same name, and decorate your place with "snow." An even more original party would involve having everyone dress as their interpretation of Santa.

Invitations
Remember that the invitation sets the mood for the party. An engraved invitation with a foil lining and R.S.V.P. card implies a very formal affair. A mimeographed sheet tacked to a bulletin board suggests an informal one. The trendiest invitation today is sent via facsimile. You may wish to indicate formal or casual dress on the invitation.

Menu
Plan the menu beforehand. A buffet for

Show off your luscious Christmas cookies by pre-senting them in baskets lined with white lace. Combine all different shapes and types. And make plenty of them— at a party, cookies are easier to eat than slices of cake.

ten to thirty people is the simplest idea. Choose foods that can be prepared ahead, reheated, or served at room temperature, and require only forks, or better yet, fingers.

Seasonal foods are ideal, both for taste and economics. Another easy and inexpensive possibility: Order a coldcut, antipasto, or vegetable tray from the supermarket deli. Accessorize food with a variety of sliced breads and unusual condiments and garnishes. Under no circumstances should you try a new recipe without first testing it out on your family. (See the following recipe section for ideas.)

Serve food from different places in your party room or even in different rooms. Your guests will keep moving and the spread will seem larger. Set up a drop table for dirty dishes and trash.

If offered, a bar should be self-ser-vice. Be sure to include nonalcoholic drinks—soda, sparkling water, fruit juice—as well. When a full bar is too labor-intensive and costly, a champagne punch is festive, feels like a real drink, and doesn't require expensive cham-pagne. You may just want to offer one specialty drink, such as an amaretto sour or cranberry-and-vodka, or simply beer and wine.

In any case, whenever alcohol is served it's wise to be prepared for guests who overindulge. Be sure there are des-ignated drivers and taxi-cab numbers on

hand; just in case, prepare the guest room and have appropriate items in the medicine chest.

Decorations

Traditional is always safe, and besides, Christmas comes but once a year. Team Christmas trees, wreaths, poinsettias, and other favorites with holiday scents, lighting, and music to put guests in a festive mood. Cluster your decorations around the rooms. Create unusual effects, such as setting up candles on a mantel in order of height, leading down to tiny votive lights extending to the floor. Decorate ahead of time to spare yourself last-minute nightmares.

◆ ITALIAN HOLIDAY BUFFET

All of these dishes have an Italian Christmas theme and might be used as hot-and-cold buffet offerings at a tree-trimming or other theme party. You needn't be of Italian heritage to enjoy them. If you wish, serve a large green salad at this festive buffet as well.

Antipasto Capo d'Anno
Hearty Holiday Cioppino
Olive Poppyseed Braid
Tiramisu
Serves 8 to 10

ANTIPASTO CAPO D'ANNO

The name of this dish translates to New Year's Antipasto. You can vary this colorful tray, if you like, with any array of red and green vegetables or herbs available in your region at this time of year. If you wish, make the fennel up to three days in advance. Bring it to room temperature before serving.

For the braised fennel:
2 large bulbs fresh fennel
2 cups strong-flavored stock (beef or chicken)
1 cup sherry *or* ½ cup dry red wine and ½ cup sweet Marsala
1 tablespoon crumbled dried sage
10 marinated sun-dried tomatoes, coarsely chopped

For the remainder of the tray:
2 small melons *or* 8 medium-size anjou pears
16 thin slices imported prosciutto (from Parma)
1 pound buffalo-milk mozzarella
1 cup Italian oil-cured olives
1 head of arugula greens *or* watercress
breadsticks or Italian bread (optional)

1. Preheat oven to 325 degrees F.
2. To prepare fennel, cut off the tough green tops and slice off the root end. Remove any tough or damaged outer ribs. Wash, dry, and cut each bulb into 8 wedges.
3. Place fennel in a 4- to 6-quart baking dish combined with stock, sherry or wine and Marsala, and sage. Bake for 1 hour, turning fennel once.
4. Strain fennel and set aside to cool. (The fennel can be made up to 3 days in advance. Simply keep chilled in the refrigerator until ready to assemble.) Arrange in a small serving tray. Sprinkle with chopped tomatoes.
5. If using melon, slice each one into eighths. Remove rinds and wrap each crescent in a slice of prosciutto. If using pears, peel, core, and slice each pear into halves and wrap in prosciutto.
6. Cut the mozzarella into cubes and toss in a small serving bowl with the olives.
7. To assemble the antipasto, select a 2-foot-diameter aluminum serving tray (available at supermarkets). Place the fennel and cheese bowls in a corner, spread the arugula or water cress around the rest of the tray. Place the melon or pears and prosciutto in decorative fashion. If serving this as an appetizer before bringing out the other dishes, serve with breadsticks or basket of Italian bread.

HEARTY HOLIDAY CIOPPINO

Italians love to prepare all types of seafood at Christmas time—from baccalà (salted cod) to scungili (octopus) and calamari (squid). Some households hold to a tradition that requires as many as thirteen different types of seafood on Christmas Eve. This hearty fish stew originated with the Italian fishermen. It now has as many interpretations as there are fishermen. This one uses a lot of shellfish, but you can vary the fish you use depending on availability and preference. The basic stock of this stew can be prepared up to three days before your party.

½ cup olive oil
2 medium-size onions, chopped
5 cloves garlic, minced
2 sweet red peppers, seeded and chopped
3 pounds plum tomatoes (use canned if fresh not available), coarsely chopped
2 cups fish stock or clam juice
2 cups dry red wine
one 6-ounce can tomato paste
2 bay leaves
1 tablespoon sugar
1½ teaspoons salt
¼ teaspoon crushed red pepper flakes
1 teaspoon ground fennel seeds
½ cup chopped fresh Italian parsley
¼ cup chopped fresh basil
1½ pounds sea bass, cut into 1-inch pieces
1 pound scallops
1 pound uncooked medium-size shrimp, peeled and deveined
1½ pounds medium-size clams, scrubbed clean
½ pound lump crabmeat
½ pound lobster meat

1. In a large heavy-bottom soup pot, heat olive oil. Add onions, garlic, and peppers and cook until vegetables are tender, about 7 minutes.

2. Stir in tomatoes, stock or clam juice, wine, tomato paste, bay leaves, sugar, salt, pepper flakes, fennel, parsley, and basil and continue cooking over moderate heat for another 30 minutes. (You can prepare recipe up to this point 2 to 3 days in advance. If you do so, store covered in refrigerator and reheat before using.)

3. Turn heat down and add sea bass, scallops, shrimp, and clams. Place lid on pot and cook about 7 minutes. Add crab and lobster and cook another 5 minutes. Serve hot with Olive Poppyseed Braid (recipe follows).

♦ OLIVE POPPYSEED BRAID

This coarse peasant bread is hearty enough to match the cioppino. Serve it piping hot with little bowls of extra virgin olive oil and freshly ground black pepper alongside the fish stew.

2 tablespoons yeast
1 teaspoon sugar
2 cups warm water
2 cups unbleached white flour
2 cups whole wheat flour
1 to 2 cups semolina flour
2 teaspoons salt
6 tablespoons olive oil
1 cup mashed pitted oil-cured olives
1 clove garlic, minced
½ cup chopped fresh Italian parsley
1 egg, beaten
¼ cup poppyseeds

1. Stir the yeast and sugar into 1 cup of the warm water and let proof until bubbly, about 5 minutes.

2. Combine the white and whole wheat flours, 1 cup of the semolina, and salt in a large mixing bowl or on a mixing board. Make a well in the middle. Stir in the proofed yeast and gradually incorporate the remaining water and 4 tablespoons of the olive oil. Use as much of the remaining semolina as needed to make a manageable dough.

3. Knead until smooth and satiny. Place dough in an oiled bowl until doubled in bulk, about 1 hour. Punch down and allow to rise another 30 to 40 minutes.

4. Prepare the filling by combining the mashed olives, garlic, remaining 2 tablespoons of the oil, and parsley. Mix well.

5. Grease a baking sheet. Punch down dough and divide into 3 equal parts. Roll each part into an oblong shape, 14 inches long by 4 inches wide. Spread 1/3 of the olive mix down the center of each oblong.

6. Roll closed into a cylinder shape—each cylinder should be about 1½ to 2 inches in diameter. Press one end of each cylinder of dough tightly together on the baking sheet, then carefully braid them, joining and pressing the opposite ends tightly.

7. Allow bread to rise until double in bulk, about 1 hour.

8. Preheat oven to 350 degrees F. Brush bread with beaten egg and sprinkle with poppyseeds. Bake about 40 minutes, until lightly golden. Allow to cool about 15 minutes before slicing.

TIRAMISU
(SICILIAN CASSATA)

This heavenly cake actually tastes better if made one to two days in advance. You can make it up to four days in advance, wrap in plastic and refrigerate.

Cake:
6 egg yolks
⅔ cup sugar
⅔ cup flour
1 teaspoon baking powder
½ teaspoon salt
6 egg whites, beaten stiff

Fillings:
2½ cups milk
1 vanilla bean, cut into 1-inch pieces
½ cup sugar
4 eggs, beaten
½ cup cornstarch
2 squares semi-sweet chocolate, melted
¼ cup creme de cacao

Icing:
1 cup heavy cream
¼ cup sugar
¼ cup creme de cacao
⅔ cup ricotta cheese
1 cup sweet Marsala

1. To prepare the cake, preheat oven to 325 degrees F. Grease and flour two 8-inch round cake pans. In a large mixing bowl at high speed, beat the egg yolks until thick and lemon-colored. At the same speed gradually sprinkle in sugar. Turn off mixer and sift flour, baking powder, and salt over egg mixture. Gently fold in egg whites, blending thoroughly.

2. Pour batter into prepared pans. Bake 25 minutes, or until top springs back when touched lightly with a finger. Use a cake tester if unsure about doneness. When cool enough to handle, remove cakes from pans.

Allow to cool completely before assembling cake.

3. To prepare the fillings, in a heavy-bottom saucepan, heat milk, vanilla bean, and sugar until sugar is dissolved. Stir a little of the hot milk into beaten eggs, then stir mixture back into saucepan and continue to cook over low heat, stirring constantly until mixture coats a spoon. Sift in cornstarch slowly to avoid lumping. (If necessary, use a hand beater to break up lumps.)

4. Cook until custard is thickened (about 15 minutes). Strain out vanilla bean pieces. This is the vanilla custard filling.

5. To make chocolate custard, in a separate bowl measure out about one third of the custard and mix until evenly blended with melted chocolate and ¼ cup of creme de cacao. If chocolate custard thins out too much, cook a little longer until thickened. Allow fillings to cool.

6. To prepare icing, beat heavy cream with sugar and ¼ cup of creme de cacao until thick. Stir in ricotta cheese.

7. To assemble, slice each sponge cake carefully into 2 layers. Place 1 layer on a cake dish and sprinkle with ¼ cup Marsala. Spread half of the vanilla custard on this layer. Place the next cake layer on top and sprinkle with ¼ cup Marsala. Spread the chocolate custard on this layer. Place next cake layer on top and sprinkle with ¼ cup Marsala Spread with remaining vanilla custard. Top with remaining cake layer and last ¼ cup Marsala. Spread icing over cake, starting with the top and working down the sides. Smooth out icing and garnish with Christmas decorations if desired.

8. Chill cake for several hours or overnight before slicing.

Sweets and Snacks for Entertaining

Here is a collection of desserts and snacks that would work well at almost any type of holiday party. All can simply be placed on a buffet table. Some are classics—such as the Maple Walnut Fudge; others, such as the Chocolate Cheese Stuffed Dates, will be a delightful new surprise for your guests.

BRANDY-SCENTED PECAN FRUIT CAKE

This is a variation on a favorite Kentucky fruit cake. Often made with bourbon, its flavor is allowed to "ripen" with time.

◆ ½ pound (2 sticks) butter
½ cup brown sugar
½ cup granulated sugar
5 eggs, lightly beaten
⅔ cup brandy
1 tablespoon vanilla
2 cups flour
2 tablespoons baking powder
½ teaspoon salt
1 teaspoon cinnamon
1 teaspoon nutmeg
½ cup golden raisins
½ cup dark raisins
½ cup currants
2 cups whole pecans
extra brandy

1. Preheat oven to 325 degrees F. Grease and flour a loaf pan.

◆ 2. Cream butter, brown sugar, and granulated sugar. Beat in eggs, one at a time. Beat in brandy and vanilla.

3. Sift together flour, baking powder, salt, cinnamon, and nutmeg. Mix in raisins, currants, and pecans. Stir dry ingredients into wet ones just until evenly blended. Pour into prepared pan. Bake for 75 minutes or until cake tester comes out clean. Remove cake from pan and cool on a rack.

4. To allow cake to ripen: Place on a plate and sprinkle with about ⅓ cup brandy. Wrap in cheesecloth. Sprinkle with a little more brandy every couple of days for about a week. Keep stored in cheesecloth in refrigerator or in a cool place.

Makes 1 loaf

CHOCOLATE CHEESE STUFFED DATES

The yogurt cheese adds an unexpected pleasant tang to the chocolatey filling. Remember to begin preparing yogurt cheese two days in advance.

½ cup Yogurt Cheese (recipe follows)
8 ounces cream cheese
3 tablespoons good quality Dutch cocoa (such as Droste)
½ cup fine sugar
4 dozen whole large pitted dates
4 dozen pecan or walnut halves

1. Beat together all ingredients, except dates and nuts.
2. Stuff each date generously with mixture and press a nut half into each. (Can be stored for up to 2 weeks in the refrigerator.)
   Makes 4 dozen

YOGURT CHEESE

one 2-pound container plain yogurt

1. Line a colander with paper coffee filters or strong paper toweling. Place the yogurt in the colander and position over a bowl or pot to catch the dripping whey.
2. Allow to drain for two days in the refrigerator, covered. Discard whey when done and store the cheese in tightly covered container.
   Makes about 2 cups

CHOCOLATE HAZELNUT BUTTER COOKIES

Use only the best cocoa for this cookie. The Dutch brand, Droste, available in specialty food stores, is one of the best.

10 tablespoons unsalted butter
⅔ cup sugar
2 eggs
¾ cup flour
¼ cup Dutch cocoa
⅓ cup ground hazelnuts
1 teaspoon baking powder
½ teaspoon salt
4 dozen whole hazelnuts

1. Preheat oven to 350 degrees F. Grease 2 to 3 cookie sheets.
2. Cream together butter and sugar. Beat in eggs, one at a time.
3. In separate bowl mix together flour, cocoa, ground nuts, baking powder, and salt.
4. Combine dry ingredients with butter mixture, stirring only until evenly blended. Drop teaspoonfuls of batter on cookie sheet, allowing plenty of space to spread. Press a whole hazelnut into the center of each cookie. Bake 7 to 10 minutes, until bottom is lightly brown. Allow to cool completely.
   Makes about 4 dozen

CRANBERRY APPLE CHUTNEY

This chutney goes well with game, root vegetables, and couscous and other grains.

4 tablespoons butter
1 large yellow onion, chopped
1 cup sugar
⅔ cup cider vinegar
½ cup water
2 tart green apples, peeled, cored, and chopped
1 teaspoon salt
½ teaspoon cinnamon
½ teaspoon coriander
½ teaspoon cardamom
4 whole cloves
½ teaspoon ground mustard
½ teaspoon ground ginger
¼ teaspoon ground cumin
1½ cups fresh cranberries

1. Heat the butter in a 4- to 6-quart saucepan. Stir in the onions and cook until soft, about 5 minutes.
2. Add sugar, vinegar and water to saucepan and stir over moderate heat until sugar is dissolved.
3. Add apples, salt, and spices and simmer for 12 minutes, stirring occasionally.
4. Add the cranberries and simmer 5 minutes longer. Store in refrigerator.
   Makes about 4 cups

FROSTY LEMON BRAZIL NUT TORTE

· · · · · · · · ·

This "frosty" cake lends itself well to Christmas decorations. After icing, decorate cake with red and green holiday candy, candied fruit, or storebought cake decorations.

1 stick unsalted butter at room
    temperature
¾ cup sugar
6 egg yolks
½ teaspoon salt
2 teaspoons grated lemon zest
2 cups ground Brazil nuts
6 egg whites, beaten until stiff but
    not dry
¼ cup lemon juice
2 cups confectioner's sugar

1. Preheat oven to 350 degrees F. Grease and flour the bottom and sides of an 8-inch springform pan.
2. Cream butter with sugar on high speed in large mixing bowl using an electric beater.

3. Add egg yolks one at a time, continuing to beat mixture on high speed. Add salt and zest.
4. Stir in ground nuts with a wooden spoon, mixing just until blended.
5. Gently fold in beaten egg whites. Pour batter into prepared pan and bake 35 minutes, or until cake tests done. Cool thoroughly before removing from pan.
6. Prepare icing by placing lemon juice in a mixing bowl. Slowly sift in sugar, whisking to incorporate smoothly. Pour icing over cooled cake, allowing it to drip down sides. Use a spatula to help spread the icing evenly. This moist cake stores very well for at least three weeks if wrapped and refrigerated.

    *Variation: A nice variation on this recipe is ground almonds instead of Brazil nuts. Also add 1/4 teaspoon almond extract. You can vary this cake with almost any nut—hazelnuts, walnuts, pecans, whatever your preference.
Serves 10

GINGERBREAD WITH LIQUEUR-SPIKED CREAM

· · · · · · · · ·

1 stick unsalted butter
¾ cup dark brown sugar
1 egg
½ cup unsulphured molasses
½ cup honey
¾ cup milk
2¼ cups flour
1 teaspoon baking powder
½ teaspoon baking soda
2 teaspoons ground ginger
¼ teaspoon salt
½ teaspoon cinnamon
½ teaspoon cloves
1½ cups heavy cream
¼ cup **Tia Maria,** *or* **Kahlua,** *or*
    Creme de Cacao

1. Preheat oven to 350 degrees F. In a saucepan, melt butter. Allow to cool, then beat it with sugar, egg, molasses, honey, and milk.
2. Grease a 9 x 9 x 2-inch pan. In a mixing bowl, blend together flour, baking powder, baking soda, ginger, salt, cinnamon, and cloves. Stir the dry ingredients into the liquid ones, mixing just until blended. Pour batter into prepared pan and bake for 55 minutes or until cake tests done.
3. Beat heavy cream with liqueur. Pour cream over individual servings of warm gingerbread.
Serves 10–12

MAPLE WALNUT FUDGE

2 cups sugar
½ cup milk
½ cup maple syrup
4 tablespoons unsalted butter, cut into equal chunks
½ teaspoon maple flavoring
1¼ cups coarsely chopped walnuts

1. Line the sides and bottom of an 8 x 8 x 2-inch baking pan with foil. Butter the foil.
2. Butter the sides of a heavy-bottom 2-quart saucepan. Combine sugar, milk, and syrup in saucepan. Cook over moderately high heat until mixture boils. Stir constantly with a wooden spoon until sugar dissolves, about 5 minutes. Do not allow mixture to splash on sides of pan.
3. Carefully attach candy thermometer to side of pan so that it is immersed in mixture, but not touching the bottom of saucepan.
4. Cook over moderately low heat, stirring frequently, until thermometer reads 234 degrees F (soft-ball stage), about 6 to 8 minutes. Mixture should boil at a moderate rate.
5. Remove pan from heat. Add butter in four pieces, and maple flavoring, but do not stir. Allow to cool to 110 degrees F, about 60 minutes. Remove thermometer.
6. Beat vigorously until mixture just begins to thicken. Add nuts and continue to beat until very thick, but still glossy, about 7 minutes. Turn fudge into the pan. While still warm, score into 1-inch squares. When firm, lift out of pan and cut into squares. Store in tightly covered container.

*Variation: To make Vanilla Walnut Fudge, substitute light corn syrup for the maple syrup and 1 teaspoon vanilla for the maple flavoring.
Makes 64 pieces

MINCEMEAT CHEESE CRESCENTS

Mincemeat can be overwhelmingly sweet and spicy for some people. This recipe tones down the cloying aspects by omitting the sugary sweet candied fruit. It uses a nice buttery cheese dough as a pleasant foil for the rich filling.

Pastry:
2½ cups flour
1 teaspoon salt
2 sticks butter, at room temperature
1½ cups creamed cottage cheese
1 teaspoon vanilla

Filling:
1 tart apple, peeled and cored
1 cup golden raisins
½ cup currants
zest and juice of 1 whole orange
2 cups walnuts
½ cup brown sugar
1 stick butter
½ teaspoon salt
2 teaspoons cinnamon
½ teaspoon nutmeg
¼ teaspoon mace
¼ teaspoon coriander
½ cup brandy, rum, whisky, or sherry
1 egg white, lightly beaten

1. Combine flour and salt in mixing bowl. Cut in butter until mixture resembles coarse cornmeal.
2. Add cottage cheese and vanilla. Mix until dough is smooth. Divide dough into 6 balls and refrigerate overnight or longer.
3. To prepare filling, combine apple, raisins, currants, orange zest and juice, and walnuts in a food processor or grinder. Process until mixture is the texture of chunky applesauce.
4. Heat mixture in a heavy-bottom saucepan. Stir in sugar, butter, salt, spices, and liquor. Cook over medium heat for about 10-15 minutes, until mixture is slightly thickened. Cool to room temperature before filling pastry.
5. Preheat oven to 350 degrees F. Grease cookie sheets.
6. To make cookies, roll each ball of dough until ¼-inch thick. Using a cookie cutter or overturned drinking glass, press out 3-inch-diameter circles of dough. Fill each circle with a heaping teaspoon of mincemeat and spread it across the diameter. Fold circles in half to close up. Crimp edges together with fork. Roll scraps and punch out circles until dough is used up. Place crescents on prepared cookie sheets and brush with egg white. Bake for 10–15 minutes, until lightly golden.
Makes 4–5 dozen.

YULE LOG WITH MOCHA CHIP FROSTING

You can dress this log up or down. Use commercial red and green decorations or color your own icing and decorate it.

Cake:
6 egg yolks
⅔ cup sugar
⅔ cup flour
1 teaspoon baking powder
½ teaspoon salt
6 egg whites, beaten stiff
powdered sugar

Frosting:
¾ cup milk
⅓ cup very strong brewed coffee
½ cup flour
2 sticks butter
¾ cup sugar
½ cup cocoa
⅔ cup small chocolate chips

1. Preheat oven to 325 degrees F. Line a 10½ x 15½ x 2-inch cake sheet with parchment or wax paper. Grease the paper.
2. In a large mixing bowl at high speed, beat the egg yolks until thick and lemon-colored. At the same speed gradually sprinkle in sugar. Turn off mixer and sift flour, baking powder, and salt over egg mixture. Gently fold in egg whites, blending thoroughly.
3. Pour batter into prepared pan. Bake 15 minutes or until top springs back when lightly touched with finger.
4. Sprinkle a cloth towel with powdered sugar. Invert hot cake with paper lining onto towel. Carefully roll up warm cake lengthwise with towel. Keep wrapped and allow to cool completely before unrolling and removing paper.
5. To prepare frosting, whisk together milk, coffee, and flour in a heavy-bottom pot. Over moderate heat cook until mixture is very thick, about 5 minutes. Place a piece of plastic wrap over surface of mixture and set aside to cool.
6. Cream together butter, sugar, and cocoa. Continue to beat until very fluffy and creamy, about 7 minutes. Beat in, at high speed, cooled flour-milk mixture. Stir in chips.
7. To ice cake, unroll and ice the inside first. Roll up tightly and ice outside.
Serves 10

SEMOLINA ALMOND PUDDING

4 cups heavy cream
1 vanilla bean, cut into 1-inch pieces
⅔ cup extrafine sugar
4 eggs, beaten
¾ cup semolina
¼ cup sweet sherry
⅔ cup ground toasted almonds
fresh fruit (optional; preferably berries)
whipped cream (optional)

1. In a heavy-bottom saucepan, heat cream, vanilla bean, and sugar until sugar is dissolved.
2. Add a little of the hot cream to beaten eggs and stir slowly back into saucepan. Continue to cook over low heat, stirring constantly, until custard is thick enough to coat a spoon. Strain out vanilla pieces.
3. Slowly add semolina, stirring to avoid lumping. Cook about 7 minutes until pudding begins to thicken.
4. Stir in sherry and almonds and blend well. Cook 5 minutes longer over low heat. Serve hot or cold, topped with fresh fruit and whipped cream if desired.
Serves 6–8

✦ SUGAR 'N SPICE NUTS

¾ cup sugar
½ cup maple syrup
1 teaspoon cinnamon
¼ teaspoon cloves
¼ teaspoon nutmeg
3 cups walnut or pecan halves

1. In a saucepan with a candy thermometer attached, combine sugar, syrup, and spices. Cook over moderately high heat until boiling, about 5 minutes. Reduce heat and cook until mixture reaches soft-ball stage (236 degrees F on candy thermometer), about 18 minutes.
2. Remove pan from heat. Add nuts. Stir briskly for about 3 to 4 minutes, until creamy. Turn nuts out onto a piece of waxed paper and separate them by hand. Allow to cool thoroughly before storing.
Makes about 2½ pounds

✦ SWEET POTATO PIE WITH GINGER AND BLANKET OF SNOW

Pastry:
1 cup whole wheat pastry flour
½ teaspoon salt
½ cup ground walnuts
½ cup ricotta cheese
1 stick unsalted butter

Filling:
2 cups mashed cooked sweet potatoes
¾ cup evaporated milk
¾ cup heavy cream
2 eggs
¼ cup brown sugar
¼ cup white sugar
1 tablespoon finely grated fresh ginger
½ teaspoon cinnamon
¼ teaspoon cloves

Topping:
1 pint heavy cream
2 tablespoons extra fine sugar
¼ cup brandy
¼ cup sour cream

1. To make the pastry, toss all pastry ingredients together in a mixing bowl and blend well with a wooden spoon or fork. Chill for 1 hour or longer. Preheat oven to 450 degrees F. Press dough into 9-inch pie plate. Place in oven and turn down to 400 degrees F. Bake for 8 minutes.
2. To prepare the filling, beat together all the filling ingredients. Pour into slightly cooled pie shell. Bake at 400 degrees F for 15 minutes. Turn oven down to 350 degrees F and bake for 45 minutes, or until an inserted knife comes out clean.
3. To make the topping, beat heavy cream with sugar and brandy until soft peaks form. Add the sour cream and beat until evenly incorporated. Top individual servings of pie with a blanket of cream.
Makes one 9-inch pie

Photography

More film is sold during the Christmas holidays than at any other time of the year, according to Kodak. It's no wonder, since photographic opportunities at this time of the year are like no other. Everyone is in a good mood and such traditional events as gift-opening and tree-trimming are naturals for catching on film. Decorated trees, stacks of presents, displays of food, and mantels hung with stockings add composition and color to photographs. Here, then, are tips for making the most of your Christmas photography:

- Shoot familiar subjects, but try to see them in a new way. Photograph someone wrapping presents rather than opening them, for example, or shoot backstage at the Christmas pageant.
- Make sure you have the nicest background available. A wall covered with Christmas cards may look cluttered, but a snow-gilded outdoor banister could be perfect.
- When taking pictures of small children or pets, crouch down to their level. If you shoot standing up, you may get only pictures of the top of a head.
- Don't waste space; fill up the viewfinder frame. Point the camera downward to move heads nearer to the top of the frame. Move in a step or two to get more of a close-up, cropping at the waist or higher or else move a step or two back to get a full figure.
- Outdoor daytime lighting is always best, but the majority of holiday pictures are taken indoors. So unless you are in a very bright house and have a high-speed film, use a flash. Move around to find the best lighting; by aiming your camera directly at windows or mirrors, you will end up with an unwanted burst of reflected light. Experiment with photographing Christmas tree lights; they're not easy subjects for amateurs.
- When you're ready to shoot, don't move. Tuck your elbows into your sides, and brace the camera against your forehead. When you push the button, squeeze it gently and in a smooth motion. Don't jerk.
- When you are taking flash pictures of more than one person, take two or three frames for every shot. It will improve your chances of getting good facial expressions and a photograph you can be proud of for years to come.

Poems and Stories

The most familiar Christmas stories, read by people year after year, were written by Clement Moore and Charles Dickens. Moore wrote "A Visit from St. Nicholas" for his children in 1922, and Dickens' Christmas books created the Victorian image of the holiday we still draw upon today. The first of the five books, *A Christmas Carol*, appeared in 1843, and was followed, one each year, by *The Chimes*, *The Cricket on the Hearth*, *The Battle of Life*, and *The Haunted Man*.

Washington Irving is also credited with his contribution to literature with a Christmas theme. Three of his essays and stories from the *Sketch Book*, issued in parts in 1819–1820, were devoted to English Christmases. Along with *Bracebridge Hall*, *Sketch Book* was warmly received in both England and America. The stories have been reprinted frequently in a variety of editions.

Hans Christian Anderson ("The Fir Tree," "The Little Match Girl"), Herman Melville ("Merry Christmas"),

Henry Wadsworth Longfellow ("The Three Kings," "Christmas 1863," "Christmas Carol"), Louisa May Alcott ("A Hospital Christmas"), Bret Harte ("How Santa Claus Came to Simpson's Bar"), Harriet Beecher Stowe ("Betty's Bright Idea"), and O. Henry ("The Gift of the Magi") are among the other well-known authors and poets of the 1800s and early 1900s who explored Christmas as a theme. Frequently, as in the case of Longfellow's "I Heard the Bells on Christmas Day" and Edmund H. Sears' "It Came Upon a Midnight Clear," Christmas poems were set to music and evolved into our best-loved hymns and carols.

Not all Christmas stories are old. Modern names linked with literature with a nativity theme include novelists and short-story writers Truman Capote ("A Christmas Memory," 1956), Pearl S. Buck (*Once Upon a Christmas*, 1972), and Garrison Keillor ("Christmas at

Lake Wobegon," 1985) as well as poets Gwendolyn Brooks ("Christmas at Church," 1965) and James Dickey ("The Christmas Towns," 1965). It would seem that as long as Christmas reawakens once a year, writers will continue to marvel at its magic with their words. (*See also Moore, Clement C.; Dickens, Charles; Carols, Christmas.*)

Poinsettia

A plant of the spurge family, *Euphorbiaceae*, the poinsettia has tiny flowers surrounded by large, colored bracts. The bracts are usually bright red, but may also be pink, yellowish, or white. Since its red "flower" so vividly contrasts with its green leaves, the poinsettia rivals holly as one of the prime Christmas plants.

Though the poinsettia is now popular all over the world, it first came to America from Mexico in 1800s. Joel Roberts Poinsett, a botanist and the first United States Ambassador to Mexico, was intrigued by this flaming red, star-shaped plant with a brilliant yellow center and brought it to his home in Charleston, South Carolina, in 1828. By the early 1830s the plant was being grown in Philadelphia; it was sold in New York's elegant shops by 1870, and in the early 1900s, flower growers in Hollywood, California, were among the first to develop and popularize the potted Christmas poinsettia.

The poinsettia gets its name from the man

who introduced it to North America, though the Mexicans call it "Flower of the Holy Night." Some say the star-shaped bracts symbolize the star of Bethlehem. A certain legend attaches seasonal significance to the plant as well: A poor Mexican boy, Pablo, picked a branch of this forest weed to offer Jesus at the shrine of the Nativity. When it was placed in front of the altar, the top leaves of the branch miraculously turned flame red, transforming the boy's gift into a beautiful flower.

Culture and Care

In tropical and subtropical regions, the common poinsettia (*Euphorbia pulcherrima*) thrives outdoors, but in cold climates it must be grown indoors. As a potted plant, it grows from one to four feet tall. Poinsettias bought at Christmastime can retain their beauty for many weeks. Place the plant in the sunniest corner of the room; avoid cold drafts from windows or doors or excess heat from televisions or heat ducts. The temperature should not exceed 70 degrees or drop below 50. Water the plant when the soil feels dry; make sure a small amount of water drips through the bottom of the plant's container. If the plant came wrapped in colored foil, punch a hole in the bottom and place a saucer beneath it to protect your furniture and floor from water.

If you plan to keep your poinsettia after Christmas, feed it every month with 20-20-20 fertilizer. Allow it to grow in a sunny window; keep temperature constant and soil moist. After blooming, cut stems back to two leaf buds, reduce water, and keep cool. Set outside in spring in a sunny spot when danger of frost is past. Potted poinsettias rarely bloom again unless they are in a greenhouse, where temperature and light can be controlled, so don't be too disappointed if your plant doesn't see another Christmas.

The festive poinsettia brightens homes, offices, restaurants, and other public places all over North America at Christmastime. In San Diego, the annual Poinsettia Festival pays further tribute to this Mexican beauty.

Rose, Christmas

Three types of "roses" have been considered as special Christmas plants. The Rose of Jericho (*Anastatica hierochuntica*), a member of the mustard family, is a small annual plant whose dried leaves and flowers open up when moistened. Generations of monks believed the plant symbolized the opening and closing of Mary's womb, and thus it became associated with Christmas.

The black hellebore (*Helleborus niger*), which is more commonly known as the Christmas rose, has white-and-green flowers and black, poisonous roots. Its ties with the season are attributed to the plant's "miraculous" appearance from the bare earth at midwinter. Like the Rose of Jericho, the black hellebore was popular until the mid-nineteenth century, when Christmas rose farms grew these plants in quantity. Finally, a treasured Christmas flower is the snow, or Winter rose, which blooms only in the Northern regions of Central Europe.(*See also Poinsettia, Ivy, Holly.*)

Rudolph the Red-Nosed Reindeer

The story of the little reindeer who leads Santa Claus's sleigh was written in 1939 by Robert L. May, a copywriter for Montgomery Ward. When May was assigned to write a children's booklet as a promotional giveaway, he created the tale of a reindeer whose nose was "red, very large, and quite shiny," whereas "most reindeers' noses were brownish and tiny."

The story became so popular that it inspired a song and an animated television special. Today children automatically add a ninth reindeer to the list of eight in Clement C. Moore's "A Visit from St. Nicholas." (*See also "A Visit from St. Nicholas"; Television.*)

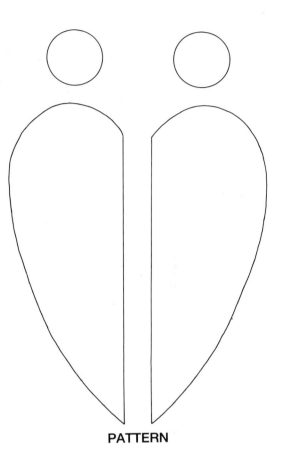

PATTERN

REINDEER HOOVES SHIRT

Here is a fun project for teenagers to make in quantity for their friends and relatives. It can be used on sweatshirts as well as T-shirts, depending on the climate where you live.

Materials:
1 piece carbon paper or substitute
1 piece of oaktag (file folder paper)
 about 4 by 6 inches or more
scissors
light-colored T-shirt or sweatshirt
cardboard to fit inside the shirt
newspaper
stencil brush
stencil paint
scribble paint (in one color for writing)

1. Using carbon paper or tracing paper, transfer the pattern of the reindeer hoof onto the oaktag paper. Push point of scissors into the middle of the hoofprint, then carefully cut out the shape of each side of the hoof. You have created a stencil.

2. Place the large piece of cardboard into the shirt to serve as a hard surface and to separate the two layers of the shirt. Lay a piece of newspaper over the cardboard to prevent the stencil paint from getting on the cardboard, and carefully change it, if necessary, as you go from one motif to the next, to prevent smears inside the shirt.

3. Using a little stencil paint at a time (on a fairly dry brush), blot the paint on the stencil through the larger hoof shape until the print is filled in to your satisfaction.

Remember, real hoofprints are not all equally clear.

4. Gently brush paint lightly into the small round holes under the big hooves to show the dewclaws occasionally touching the snow. Let one side dry before doing the other side of the shirt.

5. If the shirt has a pocket, you can write "deer" or "reindeer" on the pocket in any language. Here are a few: French: *cerf*; German: *Die Rentiere*; Norwegian and Danish: *Rensdyr*; Swedish: *Ren*; Japanese: *Tonakai*.

Saint Nicholas

See Santa Claus.

Salvation Army

See Goodwill.

Santa Claus

In almost every country around the world, some time between December 5 and January 6, a man in a red coat and a white beard appears with a sack of gifts. In America he is Santa Claus, in England he is Father Christmas, and French children know him as Père Noel. But regardless of his title or even his attire, he is a holiday symbol of love.

Today's Santa Claus developed from a real person, Saint Nicholas, who lived in the fourth century. Little is known about him, except that he was Bishop of

Myra, an ancient town now located in Turkey. Legend has it that he was only a boy when he became a bishop. He was also said to perform kind and miraculous deeds and bring gifts to the needy. His connections with children stem from a legend of three boys who were murdered by an innkeeper, only to be revived by a prayer from St. Nicholas. In these legends he wore an embroidered robe and often rode a white horse.

Word of St. Nicholas's good deeds spread northward through medieval Europe. He became the patron saint of schoolboys, and the date of his death, January 6, was commemorated in various European towns. Over time he evolved into a magical figure who embodied traits of the Norse gods, who used chimneys as their doors, and of witches, who could fly. Customs changed and the saint became Father Christmas in England and Père Noel in

France. Most of these variations had beards and wore fur robes.

Other folkloric figures also provided inspiration for the modern-day Santa Claus. In prerevolutionary Russia, there was a legend of Kolyada, a girl who wore a white robe and traveled through the countryside in a sleigh with attendant carol singers. Spain's legend of Three

"Yes, Virginia, there is a Santa Claus. He exists as certainly as love and generosity and devotion exist, and you know that they abound and give to your life its highest beauty and joy. Alas! how dreary would be the world if there were no Santa Claus!"
—Francis Pharcellus Church,
The New York Sun (1897)

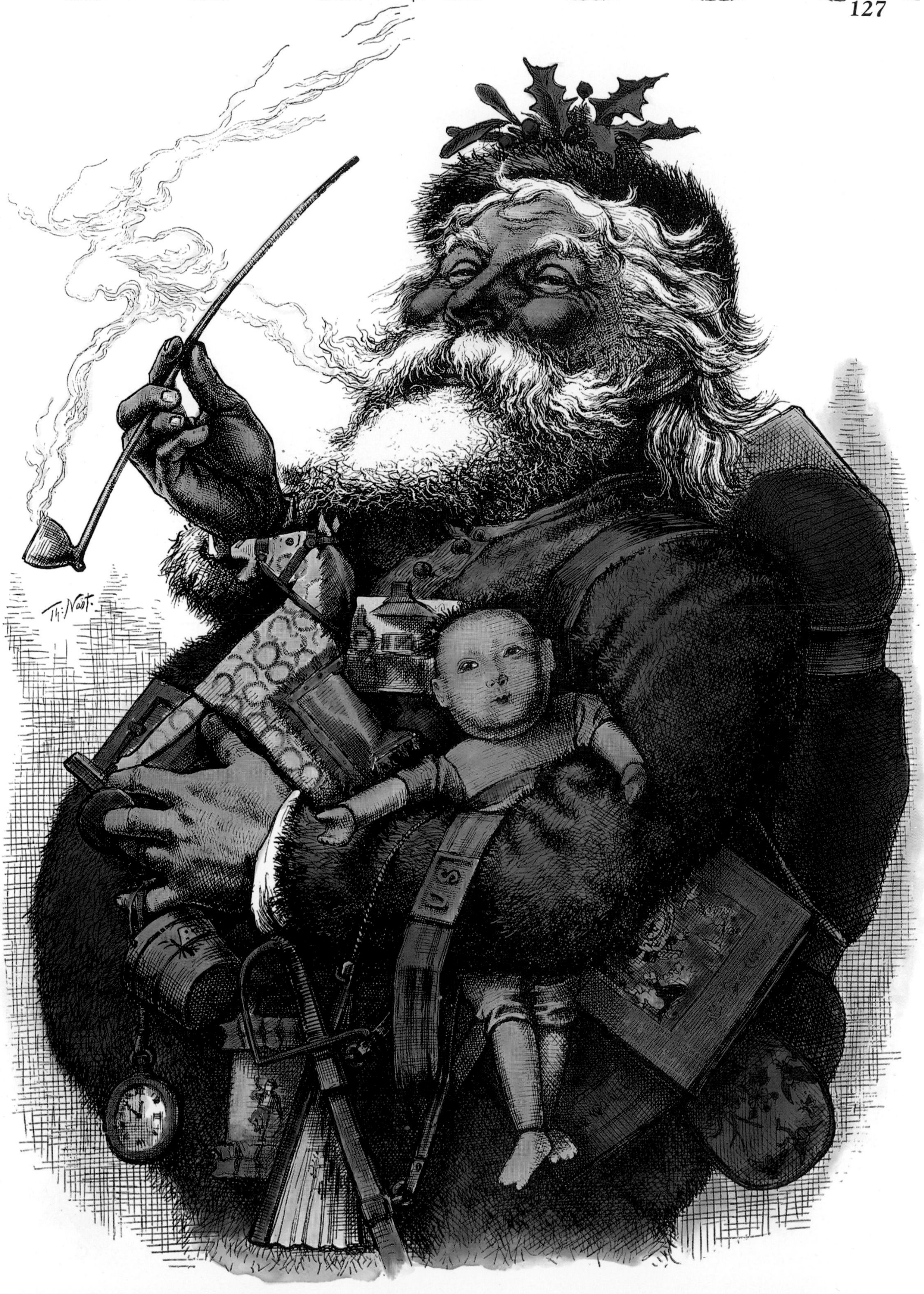
Th: Nast.

stories contributed to the image we have today of Santa Claus.

It was the Dutch, however, who gave Santa Claus his American name. The children of Dutch settlers were so fond of *Sinter Klaas* and his habit of bringing gifts over the rooftops in a horse-drawn wagon that they brought him to New Amsterdam, now New York City. English settlers eagerly borrowed the legends and festivities surrounding the kindly St. Nicholas, but when they tried to pronounce the name the Dutch gave him, it came out as "Santa Claus."

The physical image of Santa Claus today, however, originated in America. For hundreds of years Americans imagined St. Nicholas as a tall, thin person. But Washington Irving's *Knickerbocker's History of New York* (1809) created a new picture of him as a jolly fellow wearing a broad-brimmed hat and huge breeches and smoking a long pipe. In 1822 Clement C. Moore embellished the image with his poem, "A Visit from St. Nicholas." In it, the saint is pictured as a round figure wearing fur who, for the first time, rides in a sleigh pulled by eight flying reindeer.

Half a century later in 1863, political cartoonist Thomas Nast translated Dr. Moore's Santa Claus into cartoon form, which became the visual prototype of all subsequent Santas. Later, his famous drawing, "Santa Claus and his Works," which appeared as a Christmas picture in *Harper's Weekly* in 1866, showed Santa in his workshop with his record of the good and bad deeds of all children.

By the turn of the century Santa drawings were cropping up everywhere. Like St. Nicholas's robe, Santa's suit was now colored red and trimmed with white ermine fur. With the first Santa painted for a Coca-Cola advertising campaign in 1931, Santa became fatter, even larger than life. Through the years

"Frankincense to offer have I; Incense owns a Deity nigh: Pray'r and praising all men raising. Worship Him, God on high."
—*"We Three Kings of Orient Are," John H. Hopkins (1857)*

Kings who give gifts of gratitude when Spanish children leave out straw for their camels no doubt inspired the idea of leaving Santa a plate of cookies or other treats. In Germany an angelic messenger known as the Christ Child, or *Christkindl*, was said to announce Jesus's coming. In time Christkindl became Kriss Kringle and took on characteristics of St. Nicholas. All of these he's been pictured riding in his sleigh behind his newest reindeer, Rudolph, and even traveling about in his airplane and car. Early Santas often smoked a pipe, but he gave up tobacco in the 1980s. Santa might even be a little thinner these days.

Even though everyone knows that Santa lives in the North Pole, where his elves stay busy all year making toys in Santa's Workshop, at least two towns—one in Texas, the other in Indiana—have changed their names in his honor. But speaking for the children of every town—small, large, north, south, east, and west—Santa is welcome anywhere. *(See also Gifts; International Christmases; Rudolph the Red-Nosed Reindeer; "A Visit from St. Nicholas.")*

Saturnalia

Saturnalia was an ancient Roman festival given in honor of Saturn, the Roman harvest god. It began on December 17 and lasted for seven days. Schools and businesses were closed, slaves were freed, courts of law were closed, and criminals were spared punishment. At the same time, families visited, ate together, and exchanged gifts.

Saturnalia influenced centuries of subsequent midwinter celebrations in other cultures as well. This time of year—when the hours of sunlight begin to increase—seemed right for recognizing the waning of the winter season and the reemergence of a new year. In the fourth century, when the Church publicly acknowledged the birth of Jesus as a holiday, it nearly coincided with Saturnalia-

type celebrations. Over time these celebrations merged into one large holiday. *(See also Commercialism; December 25.)*

Scents, Christmas

Pine, bayberry, cinnamon, baked goods, and oranges are among the most recognized scents associated with Christmas. The evergreen essence of the Christmas tree, of course, is responsible for the pine's fragrant link to the season. The delicately spicy scent of bayberry has been popular during Yuletide since Colonial days, when the berries of this shrub were used to make holiday candles. Later, superstitions about bayberry at Christmastime evolved. One held that burning bayberry candles brought good luck to a home. Another claimed that if sweethearts who were separated at Christmas lit bayberry candles, the scent would waft from one to the other.

Because the creation of cakes, cookies, candy, and other rich foods has long been a household tradition during the holidays, the smell of baked goods is also associated with Christmas. Consequently, cinnamon, nutmeg, peppermint, and other common baking spices and flavorings are frequently combined in Christmas-scented potpourris.

Oranges were once one of the few fresh fruits available during the winter months, and therefore, have traditionally been included in seasonal feasts. Oranges also make traditional gifts, whether they stud a festive fruit basket or are mail-ordered and delivered fresh from Florida. *(See also Candles.)*

Scrooge

See Dickens, Charles.

Seals, Christmas

The annual Christmas Seal campaign, a program of the American Lung Association, began in 1907 in Delaware. When social worker Emily Bissell needed to raise money to keep a small tuberculosis clinic open, she was inspired by news from Denmark of a special Christmas stamp sold to benefit needy children. Bissell designed her own stamp, showing a wreath and the words "Merry Christmas," and sold the stamps in packets.

Bissell's motto, "Put this stamp with message bright/On every Christmas let-ter/Help the tuberculosis fight/And make the new year better," helped raise ten times the amount needed to keep the hospital open and the National Tuberculosis Association was born. Today the American Lung Association still uses Christmas Seals to obtain donations. (*See also Goodwill.*)

Here's a children's game for festive parties: Purchase a package of assorted Christmas Seals and place them around the room; give a prize to the child who finds the largest number. (Be sure to lick the Seals lightly at one end only, so they can be easily removed.)

Shopping, Christmas

"City sidewalks, busy sidewalks blink a bright red and green as the shoppers rush home with their treasures." Just as in the popular holiday song "Silver Bells," Christmas shoppers and shopping are an integral part of the Christmas season.

From automobile dealerships to supermarkets, most every retail outlet in America panders to seasonal shoppers with special sales. But the stores that have become nearly synonymous with holiday shopping are the retail giants—the department stores that originated throughout the 1800s and in the first few years of the 1900s. During the last 40 of its 124 years in business, the front

George Bernard Shaw once wrote that "Christmas is forced on a reluctant...nation by...shopkeepers and the press." Yet to many keepers of the Christmas spirit, the holiday hubbub is half the fun.

windows of B. Altman & Co. drew in New York City shoppers by the droves with their merry little mechanized figures. Long before it starred with Kriss Kringle in the movie classic, "Miracle on 34th Street," Macy's of New York City enjoyed a close-knit relationship with holiday shoppers. And what would an old-fashioned Christmas in Chicago

be without a chat with Santa and lunch under the tree at Marshall Field?

Filene's of Boston, Neiman Marcus of Texas, Seattle-based Nordstrom, Eatons of Canada, and the other retail giants supply more than their fair share of Santa's bag. However, the treasure-seeker of the late twentieth century is just as likely to shop in a smaller, more specialized store, often at a mall. These store complexes not only offer America's major department-store chains, such as J.C. Penney's, The Bay, and Sears, but also smaller shops. It is a testament to the importance of Christmas shopping that from the day after Thanksgiving to the day before December 25, every mall parking lot in America is chronically congested.

Of course for many shoppers, the search for the perfect gift is not limited to the last month of the year. A few resourceful individuals capitalize on the post-season sales that may reduce the original prices by 50 percent or more. A few more manage to make wise selections throughout the year, whenever the price is right. But for the majority, every spare hour in December is reserved for combing counters and rifling through racks, dragging bags and jostling boxes, waiting to pay and paying too much. And everyone knows someone who saves (or puts off) his gift-selecting for Christmas Eve itself.

Through it all, the origin of gift-giving itself is frequently forgotten. Yet for many the hunt is half the fun, and a year without the familiar hustle and bustle of stores in a Christmas mode is hard to imagine. So for all the promise of mail-order shopping and the decline of the giant department stores, sore soles and long lines are as typical of Christmas as they ever were. *(See also Mail-Order; Commercialism; Gifts.)*

Shops, Christmas

All over the world there are shops where it's Christmas 365 days a year. These stores typically feature scores of Christmas decorations and every holiday-inspired item one can imagine. Ornaments, lights, garlands, and other tree-trimmers usually make up the bulk of the inventory, but candles, stockings, bells, wreaths, and other greenery are also sold. Nativity figurines, collector dolls, train sets, nutcrackers, music boxes, cards, gift-wrapping supplies, pot-

✦ At Christmastime, the windows of the large department stores are better than a Broadway set. Window-dressers go to great lengths (and sometimes heights) to create holiday fantasies for starry-eyed shoppers.

pourri, dinnerware, mugs, and toys of all types are other popular items.

Although Christmas shops are most numerous in resort areas, the increasing popularity of these specialty boutiques is taking them into towns all over. In fact, a sign of the times is the emergence of Christmas-shop chains—yet another indication of the commercial power of Christmas.

*"Declare to us, bright star,
if we shall seek
Him in the morning's blush-
ing cheek,
Or search the beds of spice
through,
To find him out?"*
—**Robert Herrick
(1591–1674),
Where is the Babe?**

Spirit, The Christmas

See Goodwill.

Star

One of the most fundamental symbols of Christmas is the star. After all, this celestial body has a role in the original story. According to the New Testament, the Star of Bethlehem marked the spot where Jesus lay in his manger: "Behold, there came Wise Men from the east to Jerusalem, saying, 'Where is he that is born king of Jews? For we have seen his star in the east, and are come to worship him ' (Matthew 2:1-2). There are several theories about the Star of Bethlehem. Some believe it was a comet or nova; others think it was a conjunction of planets and stars.

We honor this shiny symbol by placing it at the top of our Christmas trees and in our windows. Stars appear on wrapping paper and Christmas cards and even dictate the shape of sugar cookies. This five-, six-, or multiple-pointed figure is also featured in several Christmas carols. Perhaps the best-known eulogy comes from the song "We Three Kings."

The star has many traditional roles in other countries as well. In Poland, Spain, Italy, and Russia, the Christmas Eve feast begins as soon as the first star appears. After supper, Polish children are questioned about their religious doctrine by "Star Man," the village priest in disguise. Wrong answers are reproved; right answers are rewarded. During the Middle Ages and sometimes today, "Star Boys" in Sweden, Germany, Poland, and Lithuania sing Christmas carols and present pageants about the Magi. (*See also Symbols; The First Christmas; Wise Men; International Christmases; Carols, Christmas.*)

THREE KINGS OF ORIENT

TRADITIONAL

1. We three kings of Or-i-ent are, Bear-ing gifts we tra-verse
2. Born a babe on Beth-le-hem's plain, Gold we bring to crown Him a-
3. Frank-in-cense to of-fer have I; In-cense owns a De-i-ty
4. Myrrh is mine; its bit-ter per-fume Breathes a life of gath-er-ing
5. Glo-rious now be-hold Him rise, King and God and Sac-ri-

far Field and foun-tain, moor and moun-tain, Fol-low-ing yon-der Star.
gain; King for-ev-er, ceas-ing nev-er, O-ver us all to reign.
nigh; Pray'r and prais-ing, all men rais-ing, Wor-ship Him, God on High.
gloom; Sorrow-ing, sigh-ing, bleed-ing, dy-ing, Seal'd in the stone-cold tomb.
fice, Heav'n sings, "Hal-le-lu-jah!" "Hal-le-lu-jah!" earth re-plies.

Chorus

Oh, star of won-der, star of might, Star with roy-al beau-ty bright,

West-ward lead-ing, still pro-ceed-ing, Guide us to the per-fect light.

STAR OF WONDER

This craft version of the Star of Bethlehem can be a simple and old-fashioned ornament for the Christmas tree or it can be used in mobiles or to decorate indoor wreaths. Its long tails can be trimmed on completion to make a simple paper star, or they can be retained on one or more sides, slit, and curled to make a believable comet, in case you favor the comet theory of the Christmas Star.

It has a simple beauty when made from white paper, but when made with gold Mylar ribbon, this star is spectacular as a bow on packages or as part of a mobile. To use as a bow, do not complete the upright points on one side.

✦ Materials:
**4 pieces of wide quilling paper
(½ inch) or a roll of ¼ or
¾ inch Mylar ribbon. The size of
the star is determined by the width
of the ribbon:**

> **¼ to ⅜ inch makes a star
> suitable for earrings
> ½ inch makes a small star
> (about 2 inches across)
> ¾ inch makes a star suitable
> for dressing up packages**

**scissors
needle and thread for hanger**

✦ 1. As the size of the star is determined by the width of the ribbon, the wider the strips are, the longer they must be. Cut ribbon into four pieces, 20 inches long for wide ribbon, 11 inches long for smaller stars.

2. Fold strips in half across their width. Trim the ends on the diagonal.

3. Now interweave the four strips to form a four-way paper knot: Wrap strip B over strip A, so the fold (made in step 2) lies tightly against the doubled edge of strip A. Wrap a third strip (C) around B. The fourth strip (D) must be wrapped around strip C, with its tails trapped in the loop formed by the fold of strip A. Do this by sliding the tails of strip D through the loop from opposite sides of strip C. Pull up so that the folds of each strip are firmly against the edges of the preceding strip.

4. Fold the top layer of tails back, overlapping in a clockwise direction, and tucking the last end through the loop formed by the first. There will be eight ends coming from eight separate locations. When you face either flat surface of the knot, four of these will be lying above the other four. That is, you will be able to see the same strip both within the knot and as a tail. Work with these strips, as follows, then flip the knot to expose the top side of the other four.

5. Fold strip away from you at a 45° angle. Wrap strip around your finger, all the way around, and insert end back under and through the loop from which it came. Pull tight and crease. It should form a little point. (The side initially away from you should be the side that shows on the end pulled through.) It is

possible to do this step correctly and have the fold not fall right, because it is a double turn, which can come out as you do it and unravel itself. You will know this has happened if the whole thing slides neatly through the loop. Slide it back through and re-do.

6. Repeat Step 5 for strips B, C, and D. Turn over and repeat Step 5 for remaining strips.

7. Lift the four loose ends on one side and fold sharply back at a 90° angle, along the edge where they emerge from the knot.

8. From that position fold each one back diagonally (45° angle). Bring the tip around and insert under the uppermost loop as shown. Push it until the tip emerges from the opposite point of the star. (If it cannot emerge, you have folded the 45° diagonal in the wrong direction.

Study the drawing carefully and correct.) Pull this until there is a sharp stand-up point. If a point doesn't form, you have the wrong side of the strip up. Slide it out again and turn the end of the strip over.

9. Repeat Step 7 for all four ends on the top of the star. If the star is to lie flat on a package, do this on one side only. Otherwise, flip the star and repeat Steps 6 and 7 on the other side.

10. Trim the ends close to the points of the star. Optionally, leave the tails on one side and curl, or split and curl.

11. To hang, use a needle to poke a thread through one of the points and tie a loop.

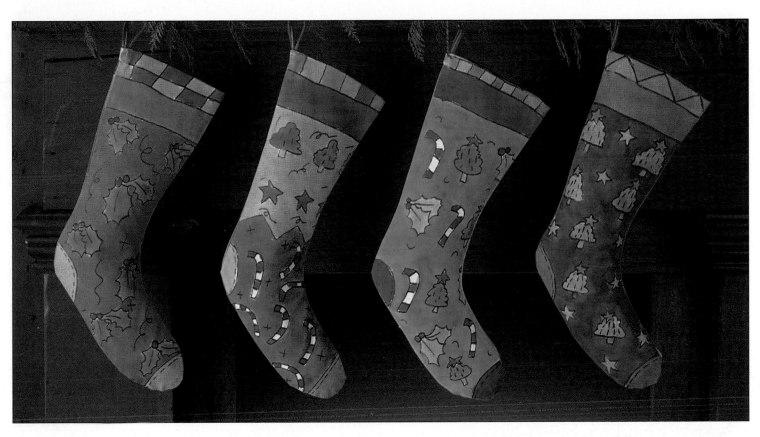

Stockings, Christmas

The custom of hanging stockings in anticipation of receiving presents originated from a story about a poor man, his three beautiful daughters, and St. Nicholas. Each of the daughters fell in love but was unable to wed because she had no dowry. When St. Nicholas, the patron saint of young people who was well-known for his generosity, heard about the daughters' situation, he anonymously threw three bags of money through the poor man's window. The bags fell into the daughters' stockings, which had been hung by the fireplace to dry.

The story of the Christian bishop's liberality spread, and today children all over the world still hang stockings for St. Nicholas to fill with fruit, candy, and small toys. (Modern stockings, however, are likely to be fancy, deco-

rated versions of the real socks that children used to hang.) The stocking tradition is observed in the United States, Australia, and New Zealand on Christmas Eve, but in many European countries children hang their stockings the night before St. Nicholas Day, December 6.

In other countries, children follow a slightly different custom. In Holland, for example, children fill their shoes with hay and a carrot for *Sintir Klaas's* white horse. The saint slides down the chimney, gathers the hay for his horse, and puts a present in each child's shoe. On January 5, Italian children set out their shoes for *La Befana*, the good witch who wanders the land bestowing gifts on all children in hopes of finding the Christ Child. (*See also International Christmases; Santa Claus.*)

Stockings

Every new Christmas magazine that appears has a new elaborately embroi-

dered or knitted Christmas stocking. Why the need to be so fancy? In many homes the Christmas stockings are a fleeting decoration, hung on Christmas Eve, gone by the next afternoon. And when the family is large, it's more important to have stockings to hang than that they be decorated with needle-point or cross-stitch.

In fact, all that is really required of Christmas stockings is that they look like Christmas, that they hold a good bounty of small presents and that they are able to survive the onslaught of children on Christmas morning. These will do all three.

Here are stockings from two families—a lined Christmas stocking with plenty of room, and two stockings made of felt or outing flannel. Both varieties can be made up in a twinkling and in quantity for that rush of children, sons- and daughters-in-law, and grandchildren on Christmas Eve.

LINED STOCKING

Materials for one stocking:
newspaper (for pattern)
½ yard of 36-inch-wide green, red or white felt
½ yard of 36-inch-wide red cotton print
13 inches ¾-inch-wide ruffled lace
¾ inch plastic or brass curtain ring
scissors, pins, green thread, and hand-sewing needle or sewing machine

1. Draw a stocking shape on a piece of newspaper. It should be at least 6¼ inches wide at the top; 12½ inches from top to heel, 11½ from heel to toe, and about 4¾ inches measured across the instep.
2. Fold the felt in half, and pin the pattern to both layers. Cut out the stocking. Pin the two sides together. Cut the red cotton print fabric according to the same pattern but *adding four inches extra at the top*, where it will be turned down to show. Pin the two sides together, *right sides facing.*
3. Sew the felt stocking together with a narrow seam allowance. Trim excess fabric closely.

4. Sew three sides of the lining, right sides facing. Sew the lace ruffle to the edge of the top. As you do so, turn the raw edge under the lace. Leave right sides facing.
5. Insert the printed cotton lining into the green felt stocking. The print design should be visible on the inside of the stocking. Fold the extra length of the lining down over the raw edge of the felt.
6. Sew a curtain ring to the top of the back, going through all layers.

PLAIN AND SIMPLE
GRAMMA'S STOCKINGS

Materials for one stocking:

newspaper (for pattern)

⅝ yard, 36-inch-wide, red or
white outing flannel (This will
make two of the large stockings.)

12 inches of ricrac*, woven braid, or
bias tape *for each round of
decoration*

plastic ring, safety pin, or 3 inches of
leftover bias tape for hanger

thread to match outing flannel

scissors

sewing machine or handsewing needle

straight pins

1. Cut a pattern to these approximate
   dimensions in step one for Lined
   Stockings (page 140). Or, for babies
   and pets, use the smaller dimensions.
2. Fold the fabric and lay pattern on
   fabric with the center back of the leg
   along the fold. Cut out one or more
   at a time.
3. Turn over top edge and hem by
   machine, or turn it down enough
   that it is sewn when you apply decoration. Sew on braid, bias tape, or
   ricrac.*
4. Pin the stocking together, right sides
   facing.
5. A 4-inch length of knitted tape was
   used as a hanger on the pet/baby
   stocking, but twill tape or even a
   length of shoelace would do as well,
   or handsew on a ¾ inch brass or
   plastic curtain hook.

*Note: For Great Lakes native American
ribbonwork: Strips of satin ribbon (or bias
tape) sewn on in overlaid, successive
rows, working down from the top.
Although this kind of ribbonwork may
originally have been stitched by hand, it is
almost always machine-stitched today.
The tight, firm rows of machine stitching*

*are part of the finished effect. These are
crossed by short strips in contrasting colors, which often form such geometric
shapes as diamonds or triangles on the
background of the horizontals.*

Pin the first horizontal strip in position about three inches from the top of
the stocking, about at the hemline. The
bias tape should be right side out. Then
pin contrasting strips (about 2 inches
long), wrong side up, between the fabric
and the bias tape, with the free ends
pointing toward the top of the stocking.
Stitch the top edge of the horizontal
tape down, by hand or machine, about
¹⁄₁₆ inch inside its top edge. This sews
down the bottom edges of the short
pieces at the same time.

Fold and press the short pieces down

over the horizontal piece and pin in position the next horizontal strip, overlapping the first strip and catching the ends
of the folded-down short strips as well as
the bottom edge of the first horizontal.
Place more short strips under this second
horizontal, and repeat the stitching.

Finishing: The last horizontal strip is
sewn both along its bottom and top
edges, and is generally not crossed by
short strips. This last strip can be at the
bottom, but could also be in the middle
and could be a piece of decorative woven
braid. To end in the center, sew one or
two strips as described above, then measure carefully and work matching strips
just far enough below them to allow the
braid to cover the edges of both unfin-
ished edges. Sew down the braid about
¹⁄₁₆ inch from both its edges.

Symbols, Christmas

From the humble manger to the elaborately decorated tree, Christmas is represented by a great many symbols. For example, Santa Claus, the roly-poly character in the red, fur-trimmed suit, is a familiar sight during Christmastime in America; not only is he the star of movies and songs, he's a familiar sight in shopping malls, at parties, even on residential lawns. The poinsettia plant's festive red blooms are synonymous with December. In fact, poinsettias are not sold or displayed at any other time of the year. Less familiar symbols in the United States are the Yule log and the wassail bowl, but they, too, make annual appearances during this widely celebrated holiday. Other Christmas symbols include the star, lights, cards, gifts, mistletoe, holly, stockings, bells, and candles. (See also Bells; Santa Claus.)

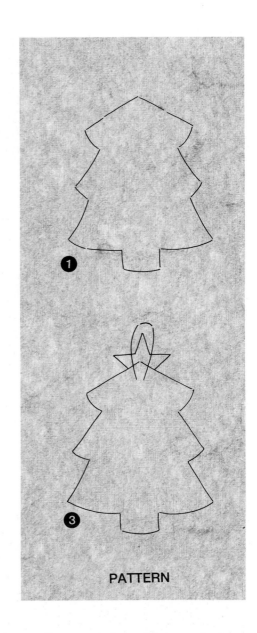

PATTERN

Festive Earrings

When Christmas is on the way, symbols of Christmas are everywhere. Lapels bloom with little wreaths, evergreen corsages, shiny balls and bells, and little mittens. Pre-teen girls fasten jingle-bells to their sneakers and women wear earrings to reflect the season.

Here are a few earrings we've seen and made. The lapel mittens are not hard to create, but they seem very tiny and are awkward to keep on the knitting needles. The result, with a red thumb, is worth the effort, however. All three designs draw on well-known symbols of the holiday season.

CHRISTMAS TREE EARRINGS

Materials:

green construction paper

red coding dots (from office supply store) or red dots from paper put through hole punch

glue

gold press-on stars

green thread

medium-sized sewing needle

2 fishhook earring backs or kidney-wire earring backs

1. Cut pattern from thin paper (or cut your own pattern freehand), trace the shape twice onto green paper, and cut out.
2. Decorate both sides with red coding dots or by gluing on dots from hole punch.
3. Place star on top. Place loop of thread as shown, crossing the sticky side of the star.
4. Place another gold star on the first, sticky sides together, carefully matching edges.
5. Put on gold fishhook or kidney wire.

CHRISTMAS STAR EARRINGS

Materials:

About 8 feet ⅜-inch-wide iridescent white ribbon

sewing needle

2 small jumprings

2 fishhook or kidney-wire earring backs

needle-nosed pliers

◆ 1. Use instruction for Star of Wonder (under "Star") to make two little stars from ribbon. Leave tails on one side, clipping and splitting them as shown.

2. Carefully pierce the tip of one point (so that tail hangs diagonally down) with a T-pin or needle, making a hole large enough to insert one end of a jump ring. Attach both star and earring back to jumpring and close with pliers.

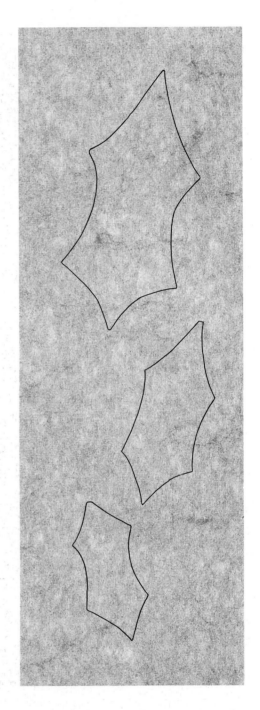

HOLLY EARRINGS

Materials:

green "cover" card or green construc-
     tion paper
green felt tip marker
needle-nosed pliers
2 fishhook earring backs or kidney-
     wire earring backs
medium-sized sewing needle
two ⅜-inch red wooden beads

◆ 1. Cut holly leaves in three sizes from
        stiff green paper, either freehand or
        using the pattern shown.
   2. Mark edges and veins with green
        marker.
   3. Make small hole in top end with a
        needle or T-pin.

◆ 4. Using needle-nosed pliers, open the
        ring end of the fishhook earring
        backs and remove the little gold
        bead and spring. Thread large,
        medium, and small holly leaves onto
        the wire, then the red bead. With
        the pliers, recreate the little ring to
        secure these.

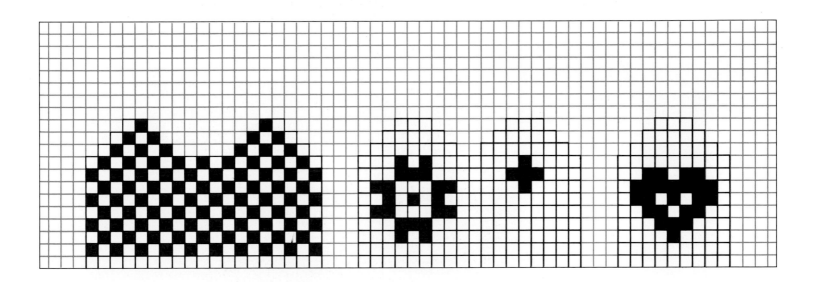

LAPEL MITTENS*

Materials:

8 yards main color sport-weight yarn
(A firm twist is helpful. Softer
yarns tend to split when knitted on
tiny needles.)

3 yards contrasting color sport-weight
yarn

3 no. 0 or 1 double-pointed needles, or
a pair of no. 0 or 1 single-pointed
needles to knit the mittens flat

yarn needle

safety pin, needle, and thread for
attaching mittens to lapel

Note: These mittens can be knitted
flat and sewn up afterwards. To knit
them flat, substitute the word purl in
the directions for knit every second
round. They look best if they are knitted circularly.

Directions: Cast on 18 stitches in
main color (mc) with 9 stitches on *two*
needles. First round: Knit around in
mc. Second round: Change to contrast
color (cc) and knit around. Third
round: Knit 1 mc, knit 1 cc around.
Fourth round: Knit around in cc. Fifth

and sixth round: Change back to mc
and knit around twice. Choose one of
the samples and knit one of the designs
on one or both sides. Do not be concerned about carrying the cc on the
back of your work, or weaving it in.
The mitten will never be worn on
a hand, and it's quite all right to have
the cc strand crisscrossing the inside
of the mitten.

When you have completed the
chart, begin decreasing at both ends of
both needles: Knit 1, slip 1, pass the
knit stitch over the slipped stitch. Knit
to 2 stitches at end of needle. Knit 2
together. Repeat this for three rounds,
then break the yarn with about a 2-foot
tail. Thread this onto a yarn needle,
and draw up the remaining stitches
firmly on the tail. Secure the tip with a
couple of stitches, then slip the needle
(and the tail) into the mitten through
its tip. Fasten the tail inside the mitten, then emerge one stitch from the
edge of the palm, at about the 9th
round. On two knitting needles, pick
up one side of 3 stitches from the 8th
round and two from the 9th round.
These will be the thumb. Knit, starting
with the 8th round. Knit 3 rounds,

then knit 2 together twice. Thread the
tail onto a yarn needle and through the
remaining 4 stitches and pull up. Run
the needle into the mitten through the
tip of the thumb. Fasten the tail with a
few stitches inside the mitten and
secure. Cut yarn.

For the second mitten, don't forget
to put the thumb on the other side of
the palm.

When both mittens are completed,
use a yarn needle to pull the contrasting
color tail through the cast-on edge of
the mitten. Use both tails from the casting on to tie the two mittens together
with a little bow. Using a sewing needle
and thread, stitch a safety pin to this
bow, stitching through it at the same
time to prevent it from coming undone.
Or, work the tails into the inside of the
mitten and sew the two mittens
together and to a little ribbon bow.

**Thanks to Lizbeth Upitis, Latvian
Mittens (Dos Teodoras, 1981) for figuring
out the technique for these mittens. The
Latvian mittens are smaller and bear different designs. Other knitters have passed this
pattern from hand to hand since her book.*

t

Tannenbaum

The German word for Christmas tree, tannenbaum is a familiar one among North Americans partly because the German carol "O Tannenbaum" is popular. The initiation of the word into the English language is also probably due to the fact that Germany is chiefly responsible for the popularization of Christmas trees and ornaments. (*See also Ornaments; Tree, Christmas; Carols, Christmas.*)

It has become the practice in North America to illumine evergreens on front lawns. But its true place is inside the home, where it stands a thing of wonder to the children, the Tree of Life as a symbol of Christ.

Television

The same year that the animated "A Charlie Brown Christmas" won an Emmy for Outstanding Children's Program, "The Bob Hope Christmas Special" won for Outstanding Variety Special. So it happens that since 1965 Christmas has been very, very good for television.

In fact, Bob Hope's specials, which document his live shows for American troops overseas, were television favorites long before 1964—in 1958 he won a Trustee's Award for his work. Yet his Christmas specials won wider appeal as they were aired, so that many of his shows, right up to the last one in 1972, were included in the one hundred top-rated TV specials.

Charles Schulz's Peanuts characters have appeared in many specials, but the holiday cartoon about Charlie Brown's quest for the meaning of Christmas is the best noted. The children who grew up with this extra-special special now have their own children who also wait for its annual airing.

Other animated Christmas shows have also delighted children and adults alike through the years, among them, Dr. Seuss' "How the Grinch Stole Christmas." Puppet renditions of "Rudolph the Red-Nosed Reindeer" and "The Little Drummer Boy" are holiday musts for little ones as well.

Family-style variety shows have appealed to adults for many years. "Christmas with the Bing Crosbys" (1972) and "Bing Crosby's Sun Valley Christmas Show" (1973) are included in the list of top-rated TV specials of all time. Andy Williams, John Denver, Kenney Rogers, and Dolly Parton have also contributed Christmas specials featuring singing and dancing.

Traditionally, regular primetime TV programs produce a December show with a Christmas theme. Will Geer won an Emmy in 1977 for his appearance in "Eight is Enough" show titled "Yes, Nicholas...There is a Santa Claus." Holiday airings of the award-winning "M*A*S*H" were always memorable. "The Waltons" series was actually spawned from a movie made for Yuletide programming, *The Homecoming—A Christmas Story* (1973), starring Patricia Neal and Richard Thomas. "The Brady Bunch" series of the early seventies inspired a family reunion in the TV movie *A Brady Bunch Christmas* (1988).

Besides the many films made for television, there are also classics from the big screen that have since retired to nonprimetime airing but are nevertheless indispensable. For all their years, *It's a Wonderful Life*, *Miracle on 34th Street*, and the various interpretations of *A Christmas Carol* may very well be the highlight of holiday programming. (See also Hope, Bob; Movies; Music.)

In television's animated, "How the Grinch Stole Christmas," the miser who lives on a mountaintop high above Whoville gets a lesson in Christmas spirit. Dressed as Santa Claus, he steals—and then returns—all the makings of the festivities, right down to the roast beast.

Toys

In the opinion of most children, a toy is the only gift worth its salt at Christmastime. Until mass-manufactured toys first appeared near the middle of the nineteenth century, the playthings of most youngsters were homemade. Dolls were carved from wood or sewn from old linens and stuffed with straw. Other typical hand-fashioned toys of the time include rocking horses, building blocks, and games.

By the end of the Civil War, toy shops had sprouted up by the dozens and America's gift-giving frenzy was in full swing. Shopkeepers piled high their counters with drums, hoops, dollhouses, kites, wind-up boats and trains, music boxes, and arks with precut, prepainted animals. In the South, children received "poppers" or "crackers" in their stockings—miniature firecrackers in brightly colored paper. Little girls in New York City could admire the array of fancy Christmas dolls in the toy shop windows.

Manufacturers have traditionally gone to great lengths to invent new toys that will captivate the children of the era. Some, like the electric train and stuffed teddy bear (named after President Theodore Roosevelt) of the

early 1900s, evolved into classics, as did the 1914 construction pieces known as Tinkertoys. In the twenties and thirties, little boys received hand-cranked dumptrucks and tiny cars for Christmas; little girls of the forties played with dolls modeled after celebrities.

Mr. Potato Head—a set of eyes, ears, noses, and mouths that gave this everyday vegetable its own personality—first came on the market in 1952. A fashionable doll with an hour-glass figure named Barbie was introduced in 1959. All manner of battery-operated and electronic toys became popular in the sixties and seventies.

Today the newest, most exciting toys are computer-run. Video games, for instance, have generated millions of dollars of revenue for their companies. Animated television shows and popular movies consistently inspire "action figures"—moveable dolls primarily for boys—while toy cars get faster, sleeker, and more sophisticated. Dolls marketed for little girls continue to be popular, even as they come and go. In 1984 and 1985, the funny-faced Cabbage Patch Kids were all the rage. Even though they were relaunched in 1989 after an absence from the toy-store shelves, it was Barbie, this time in her Happy Holidays attire, who stole the show. (*See also Crackers, Christmas; Gifts; Children.*)

✦ JUMPING JACKS

Here are two versions of the old-time jumping jack—good for filling stockings or hanging by a doorway. If the Christmas bustle is getting you down, pull the string and your little hand-made friend will cheer you with his exuberance.

One design is made of corrugated cardboard with fastenings of plastic button posts. These are easier to cut out and finish but not as strong as the wooden ones, sawn with a coping saw from wide, spruce lattice stock and fastened with bits of 18-gauge copper wire. The wooden ones will hold together even when yanked by a two-year-old.

Note carefully the positions of the two holes. The hole for the button post is the pivot point for the limb in question; the holes for the strings on each pair of limbs should be fairly far apart and high so that when you pull down on the string, the limbs will fly up. Give a little thought to the physics of it to avoid disappointment.

✦

PATTERN

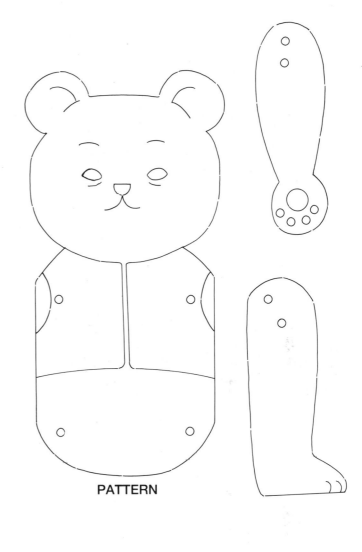

PATTERN

Materials:
tracing paper or carbon paper
scissors
tempera or other paint
finely twisted, strong string
small rubber bands (the kind that
    come around the scallions)

For cardboard jumping jacks:
- light, stiff corrugated cardboard
- paper fasteners
- a flat object $\frac{1}{8}$ inch thick for a
  spacer
- a leather, or other adjustable, punch

✦ **For wooden jumping jacks:**
- $1\frac{1}{2}$ inch to $1\frac{7}{8}$-inch-wide lattice
  stock. Four feet is about the least
  you can buy in the lumber yard.
  Balsa wood is not an acceptable
  substitute as it is too lightweight.
- 20- to 22-gauge copper wire
- needle-nosed pliers
- coping saw
- drill bit, about $\frac{1}{16}$ inch

1. Use carbon paper or tracing paper to
   transfer pattern to $1\frac{3}{4}$-inch-by-
   $\frac{1}{4}$-inch lattice stock or corrugated
   cardboard. The grain of both should
   run the length of the pieces. (If you
   wish, make your own design directly
   on the material using the patterns as
   a guide.)

✦ 2. Cut out with scissors for cardboard
   or coping saw for wood. For both,
   avoid turning inside corners. Instead,
   cut in toward the corner from two
   directions. Don't punch or drill
   holes yet.

3. Sand wood pieces. Paint fronts and
   sides of all pieces. Allow to dry. Punch
   or bore holes, making sure that the
   ends labelled A don't meet when the
   arms (or legs) are raised. Use a small
   diameter punch (a leather punch
   offers choices). A $\frac{3}{16}$-inch punch is
   perfect for standard paper fasteners.
   For wood, use a $\frac{1}{16}$-inch bit.

4. Attach arms together with a rubber
   band looped through the top hole
   of each arm. Attach legs together
   the same way.

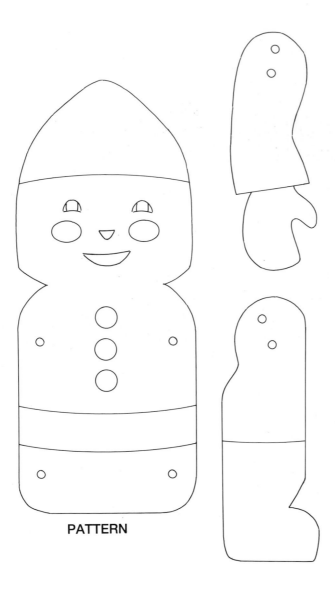

PATTERN

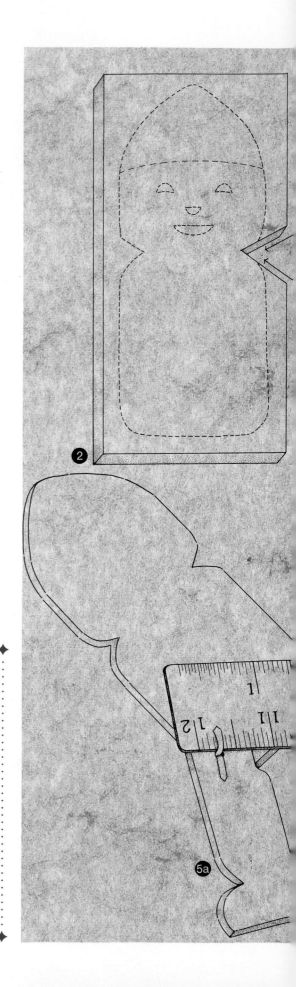

5a. Cardboard: Lay head and body piece face down with paper fasteners sticking up through them. Place leg and arm assemblages on top, front sides down. Press a firm edge, the spacer, up to each leg of the paper fastener before bending. The legs must hold the layers firmly but loosely together, so that the limbs will fall back in place after they're raised. Fasten all limbs in place.

5b. Wood: Using 20- or 22-gauge copper wire, thread an end through both layers, and twist it in a small circle around tip of needle-nosed pliers. Turn Jack over, use the cut-

ters on the pliers to cut the wire ¹/₂ inch above the wood, and twist this into another little circle around the tip of the pliers. Do this with all four joints. Attach with rubber bands, as in step 4.

6. Tie a string from the center of the top rubber band to the bottom rubber band, as shown above, letting 8 to 9 inches dangle from between its legs. Tie a loop in the bottom.

7. Punch or bore a small hole at the top of the head. Thread a piece of string through and tie it in a loop.

8. Hang up against a wall. Pull string. Smile.

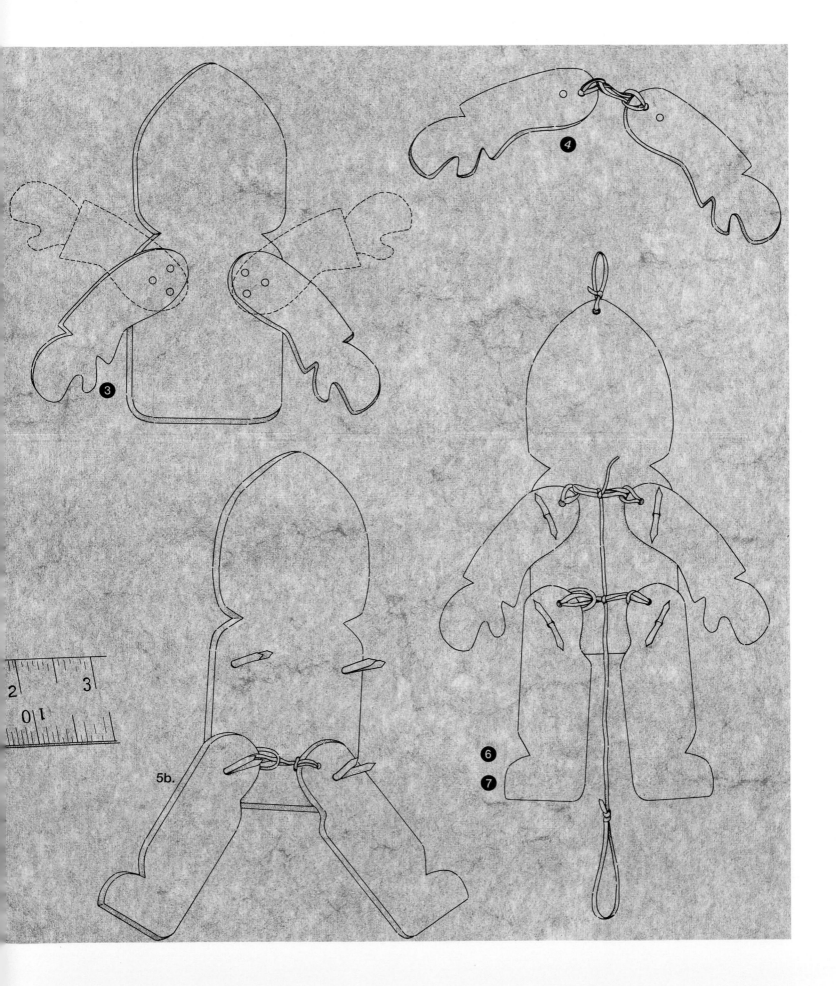

3

4

5b.

6

7

Norway Spruce

Balsam Fir

Three Kings

See Wise Men.

Tree, Christmas

Among the symbols of Christmas, the tree is one of the most important. It's been estimated that two-thirds of the homes in the United States center their holiday festivities around this decorated tradition. Families in Canada, Germany, and other parts of Europe pay tribute to the festive evergreen as well. Although the contemporary tree may be artificial, garnished with electric lights, and exploited by North American commercialism, its story is old and humble.

History

Long before the tree was a part of Christmas, it was a symbol of hope and joy. In fact, the use of evergreens was closely associated with ancient pagan ceremonies. Trees were decorated at Saturnalia, the ancient Roman festival. In Northern Europe, the Druids honored their chief god by tying tributes to tree branches. With the advent of Christianity, evergreen trees began to lose their association with pagan rituals and became part of Christian festivals, symbolic of the new life brought to the world by Jesus after the long, dark days of winter.

There are many stories concerning the first Christmas tree. One legend relates how the tree was shown in a mir-

acle to an English missionary named Winfrid, later called Saint Boniface. According to another legend, Martin Luther, a founder of the Protestant faith, was the first to bring home a cut fir tree and to place candles on its branches. As for the earliest historical references, Christmas trees were decorated with artificial roses in the Soviet Union during the sixteenth century before they were set afire.

Yet the Germans most often are credited for the development of the Christmas tree tradition. In 1605 a visitor to Stasbourg wrote of fir trees set up in parlors and decorated with paper roses, apples, wafers, candies, and sugar. It is thought that the custom spread from Stasbourg throughout Germany

White Pine

Blue Spruce

and on to Finland, Denmark, Sweden, Norway, England, and other European countries by the nineteenth century. England, for example, quickly took to the notion when Prince Albert set up and decorated his country's first Christmas tree in 1841.

The first records of a Christmas tree in the United States also date back to the nineteenth century. An 1825 edition of the *Saturday Evening Post*, for example, described decorated trees throughout the city of Philadelphia. By the 1890s, American toy importers were bringing in ornaments from Germany and the Christmas-tree custom became firmly established in this country.

✦ Types of Trees

Different varieties of trees have been used to celebrate Christmas over the years. Many of the legends about Christmas trees feature a fir. A number of old accounts and early photographs of Christmas trees show hemlocks, although their use was relatively small since the ends of a hemlock's branches are too frail to support most ornaments. Actually, cedar trees were popular up until the 1860s, but by 1880 other evergreens were chosen because they were less of a fire hazard.

Today at least fifty different kinds of conifers are sold as Christmas trees in the United States and Canada, and as many as six may be available on a single lot. The most common types are

✦ pines, spruces, and firs. The balsam fir, which grows in the northeastern part of the United States, is considered the classic Christmas tree; it has horizontal, rigid branches and an ideal, pyramidal shape. Despite its name, the Douglas fir is not a true fir, but its fragrant, straight, bright-green needles, densely set along the branch, make it a favorite in the Pacific Northwest. In the South, a much-favored tree is the Virginia pine, which is similar to the Scotch pine, another popular tree with stiff, slightly twisted needles, sturdy boughs, and dense, long-lasting foliage. Other common choices in this country include the Norway spruce, red spruce, black spruce, white pine, and the red pine.

Choosing and Caring for a Tree

When you've seen one Christmas tree, you haven't seen them all—the industry is a bustling one in this country, and it's important to get your money's worth. First measure the ceiling height and floor area where the tree will be placed. Then decide between a cut tree and a live one. A live tree, such as a white pine or potted hemlock, can stand being indoors for only a week, so it must be cared for outdoors until just before Christmas. Make sure the root ball is intact and moist when purchased. Many people replant their live trees after use. If you wish to plant the tree a few days after Christmas, in colder climates it may be wise to dig a hole in the autumn before the ground freezes. Otherwise, find a sheltered spot for storage and pack the root ball in straw until the ground has thawed.

When selecting a cut tree, look for one with a healthy, deep-green color—yellowing is a sign of dryness. There are two basic tests for freshness as well. First, bend one needle gently between your thumb and forefinger. If it's flexible, it's acceptable; if it's brittle and breaks, it's probably not fresh. Now, grasp the tree around the trunk and shake it slightly; a fresh tree will shed a few inside needles but not its outside needles. Also look at the bottom of the stump; a wet and sticky one indicates a freshly cut tree.

Whether the tree is cut or live, locate it away from fireplaces or other heating sources that will cause premature drying. Set the live tree's pot in a galvanized tub or other waterproof container. Remember to water frequently

♦ *In the early days of the Christmas tree, it was the custom to place gifts on the branches rather than beneath them. From her perch on a glistening tree branch, this doll ornament pays tribute to the custom.*

so roots stay moist, but not saturated.

If you plan to keep a cut tree for more than a week, make a fresh cut across the trunk about one to two inches from the end. Immediately place the stump in water. Use a bucket or tree stand that is large enough to hold at least one to two cups and up to a gallon of water. Check the water level every day and replenish frequently.

Artificial trees, of course, require

very little maintenance or care. What's more, they're economical—an artificial tree may cost only slightly more than a live one and can be packed and unpacked year after year. Although the higher-quality artificial trees are quite convincing, traditionalists complain that they don't have the same charm or aroma as a real tree.

Decorating a Tree

For many, the trimming of the tree is a traditional event held days or even weeks before Christmas Eve. Some families designate a special date and allow everyone to participate. For some people, trimming the tree is also an excuse to throw a party. For others it is a tradition to quietly decorate the tree in the wee hours before Christmas morning, much to the delight of the sleeping children who awaken to find it magically transformed.

In any case, there are some basics to creating a well-dressed, traditional, indoor tree. Once the tree is secure in its stand, give some thought to the electric lights, if you plan to use them. Most trees feature a rainbow of colors, but for a more elegant look, consider creating a color scheme. Two-color arrangements, for example, are attractive when one color predominates and the second accents. Try green with red accents or blue or green with white accents. One-color trees are just as intriguing; an all-blue scheme, for example, conjures an image of a cold, frosty night. Pink is sweet and gentle, but all red or all yellow makes a tree look brown. There are a variety of electric lights to work with, such as the miniature twinkles and the old-fashioned candelabra types.

Typical of big-city Christmas atmosphere are the festivities in New York City, where decorations begin to appear even before Thanksgiving. Here are the Christmas trees at Rockefeller center (opposite page); Christmas shows like the New York City Ballet company's production of **The Nutcracker Suite;** *the sparkling row of lighted trees along Park Avenue; and the 75-foot star atop the Pan Am building are only a few of the sights and sounds.*

Before you "string" the tree, check the lights for safety first. (See Lights, Christmas.) Then begin work from the top down. Lights can be strung in a wave pattern (in scalloped, horizontal lines from the tip of one large branch to another, which allows them to droop slightly between); conical pattern (straight from the top on guide wires, which are looped around the tip of the trunk, drooped, and staked to the ground); or solid pattern (hung randomly until there are no blank spots).

Next, arrange strings of garland, bells, popcorn, cranberries, or chains around the tree in a circular fashion. Hang or secure ornaments on individual branches—of course, choices depend on tradition and preference. Most families, for example, look forward each year to unpacking the miscellaneous assortment of ornaments collected and handed down from generation to generation. But if you don't boast such an heirloom collection, decorate a tree with just stars or silver balls; with fishing tackle and equipment; with tiny mittens and baby's breath; or with any other collection that follows a theme or else strikes your fancy.

After the ornaments are secured, follow with tinsel, icicles, or angel's hair, if desired. For many tree-trimmers, the climax is topping the tree with a very special ornament, traditionally an angel or star. However, the pragmatist has been known to place the tree-topper first, even before the electric lights, since such maneuvering at heights can disturb the fragile ornaments hung below.

Unusual Decorating Ideas
- Use electric lights to decorate an evergreen or other tree on your lawn; just be sure to use waterproof lights.
- Borrow a European custom and trim an outdoor tree for the birds. Bread, cookies, orange slices, and cranberry and popcorn garlands make attractive edible ornaments.
- Instead of buying a tree, decorate any small evergreen or a houseplant such as boxwood, privet, or sweet annie (*Artemisia annua*). Use a lightweight string of lights or your smallest ornaments; experiment with ribbons tied into bows, strands of pearls, or other decorations that will accent without overwhelming your plant.
- Christmas trees aren't limited to the center of the living-room floor or to evergreens. Decorate a table or your office window seat with a mini-tree, or put your creativity to use by making a tree. No matter what form it takes, a Christmas tree brightens up most any space.

Famous Christmas Trees
Ever since 1933, a 50- to 90-foot tree has been the Yuletide center of attention at New York City's Rockefeller Center. It is believed that more persons—now in excess of 2,500,000—see this tree every year than any other. In Washington, D.C., the President annually lights a tall spruce on the White House lawn; fifty large balls symbolize each state. More than 750 lights and over 1,000 ornaments decorate a giant old live oak in Wilmington, North Carolina, at Christmastime, and sixteen Irish yew trees make a pretty annual sight in San Francisco's Union Square. (*See also Carols; Decorating; Evergreens; Lights, Electric; Tradition.*)

"Twas the Night Before Christmas"
See "A Visit From St. Nicholas."

Twelfth Night
See Epiphany.

JACOB'S LADDER

According to the Old Testament, Jacob was sleeping in the wilderness one night when he awoke and saw a great staircase extending up to heaven with shining angels ascending and descending. This story has inspired renditions of Jacob's ladder down through the centuries, from knitting and quilt patterns to tricks with newspaper and long paper ladders extending from the bottom to the tip of German Christmas trees. Some American families use ribbons extending from the foot to the top of the tree: these, too, are a form of Jacob's ladder.

When the idea of Christmas trees moved outward from Germany in the last century, they often included a Jacob's ladder and angels— odd mixture of pagan and Christian symbolism typical of Christmas. Although North Americans often top

their Christmas trees with angels, the idea of the ladder never really took hold, so North American angels have no means of descent from the top of the tree.

Here are two kinds of Jacob's ladder: a white, shining ladder cut from computer paper and a modern ladder folded of ½-inch strips of colored and white paper in the same way small children make "springs" for paper jumping jacks.

The folded paper ladder can be hung extending down the tree as a Jacob's ladder, or hung around the tree like a paper chain. It's fun to make and fun to look at and handle later. The more precision there is in the folding, the better the ladder will look and behave.

◆ **White Paper Ladders Materials:**
  5 connected sheets of white,
    8½ by 11 inch computer paper
  scissors
  transparent tape
  paper cutter (optional)

1. Cut paper lengthwise in half with scissors or paper cutter to make accordion pleated piles each 5 thickness deep 4¼ by 11 inches. Cut one or both in half again to produce piles ²⁄₁₈ by 11 inches.
2. Fold one pile in half lengthwise.
3. Cut along folded edge, cutting out first a half square, leaving about half as much between squares to form the rungs of the ladder. Unfold to full length.
4. Make at least one more. Tape the two segments together and hang from the tip to the foot of the Christmas tree. Hang ornamental angels around that part of the tree.

COLORED LADDERS
· · · · · · · · · ·

Materials:

Colored paper and white paper. It should be lighter weight than construction paper. Computer paper is fine. So is lightweight, brightly colored stationery bought by the pound at a paper store.

Scissors or paper cutter

White glue

1. Cut 2 sheets each of colored and white paper into strips ½-inch wide.
2. Glue one white end on another colored end at right angles. Hold until the glue sets.
3. Fold red over white at a right (90-degree) angle.
4. Fold white over red.
5. Keep folding one over the other without turning the work over. First graders call this "making a spring." To make a colored ladder,

make a very, very long spring. When you get to the end of the first strips, glue a new white strip to the white, a new red to the red. Hold until glue sets and continue. You can also join two colored ladders together with glue, but this can spoil the gentle spiralling effect of a continuous ladder.

6. Hang either from top to bottom of the Christmas tree as a Jacob's ladder or around the tree like garlands of a paper chain.

SNOWBALL ORNAMENTS

Those white polystyrene balls in the stores at Christmastime! People try so many ways to make them into Christmas decorations, covering them with cloth, with wrapped yarn, with felt, sticking them full of glittered toothpicks and just glitter. But they still do look a lot like snowballs.

There is a nifty way to take advantage of this snowball appearance and to make a manufactured-looking Christmas tree ball with very little effort or skill by covering the balls with white craft glue, gently pressing onto them motifs carefully separated from

✦ Christmas paper napkins, then rolling the glue-covered ball in iridescent white glitter.

Materials:

Christmas paper napkins with small motifs (those with a white background work best)
polystyrene balls (3-inch diameter is best)
white craft glue
white iridescent glitter for snow
needle and thread for hanger

✦ 1. Cut out rough motifs from napkins with some white around the edges. Avoid sharp corners. Separate the layers of paper, and use only the uppermost layer bearing the motif.
2. Paint or smear white glue all over the ball. Make only one ball at a time.
3. Arrange the motifs on the ball and smooth onto the surface gently with fingers.
4. Roll ball in glitter, or sprinkle with glitter.
5. Place on pastry rack of waxed paper to dry.
6. Pull thread through top of ball and tie into a loop for hanging.

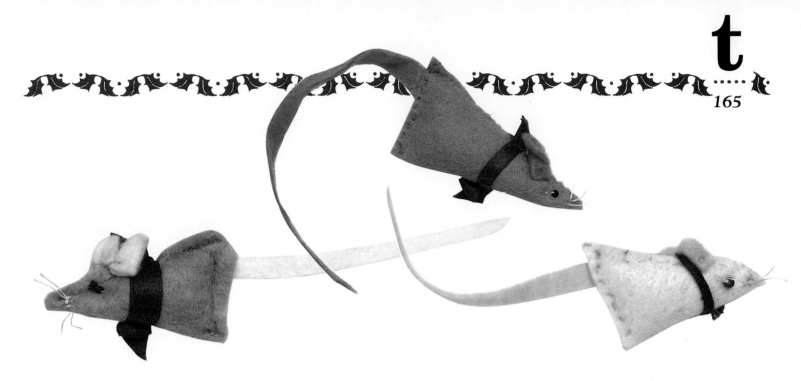

MOUSE ORNAMENTS

· · · · · · · · ·

"Twas the night before Christmas, when all through the house/ Not a creature was stirring, not even a mouse," wrote Clement Clarke Moore in *A Visit From Saint Nicholas*, and thus putting mice into the traditions of Christmas along with Santa Claus, sugarplums, and roast goose. Mice are not an old Christmas symbol, but they sure manage to sneak in whenever they can. It must be because there are so many small goodies around at Christmas. These little felt mice are meant to hang on the Christmas tree, wearing their seasonal finery. Their whiskers can be made of white or black thread or monofilament fishing line. Their eyes are shining black or red glass beads.

They are a project which children can help with, cutting the larger parts, stuffing the little bodies, even, if they are clever little craftspeople, sewing the seam along the back and later along the back end. The ears, whiskers, and bright eyes are a little harder though. Maybe an adult can finish up the job.

◆ Materials for one mouse:

mouse body: 2-inch by 2-inch piece of felt. Black, gray, white, or tan are nice mousey colors. One standard-size rectangle of felt will make many mice.

mouse tail and ears: ½-inch by 6-inch piece of felt in pink or light brown.

thread matching body color

about 1 tablespoon polyester stuffing (or felt scraps)

2 black or red seed beads

6 inches narrow satin ribbon or embroidery floss

handsewing needles, scissors: (The mice are too tiny for machine sewing to be used effectively)

Optional: fine monofilament for whiskers and hanger

1. Fold felt near an edge and cut a right triangle with a 1-inch base. Unfolded, the triangle will be 2 inches high with a 2-inch base.

2. Using a second color make the ears by cutting a rectangle ¾ inch long by about ½ inch wide. Round off the corners to make an oval. Cut in half across the width to make 2 ears. Cut tail from an edge. The tail is simply a narrow triangular strip, about ⅜ inch wide at one end, narrowing to nothing. Clip off the very narrowest part, which will otherwise fray.

3. Sew top edge of mouse's body together. Leave back end open.

4. Stuff mouse.

5. Sew the mouse's back end closed, catching its tail into the seam at the top to hold it in place.

6. Use white or black thread or fine monofilament fishing line for the whiskers. Anchor the end to the nose tip with a knot, then work back and forth, making a loop or two around a finger on each side of the face and anchoring each loop with a stitch or two inside the head. Make one or two anchoring stitches and run the needle and monofilament out through the back and snip off close to the mouse. Wiggle its skin around so that the end disappears inside. Cut the loops open.

7. With a needle and thread, sew on the eyes and ears, making a pleat in the base of the ear as it is stitched on. Anchor the thread after sewing on each part, then slip the needle inside the head to the next part. Anchor the thread after the final part and slip out through the back as in step 6. With a new thread, experiment to find the best balancing point on the mouse's back for a hanger. Tie a thread or monofilament loop to hang the mouse on the Christmas tree.

8. Tie a bow around the mouse's neck with brightly colored embroidery floss or very narrow satin ribbon.

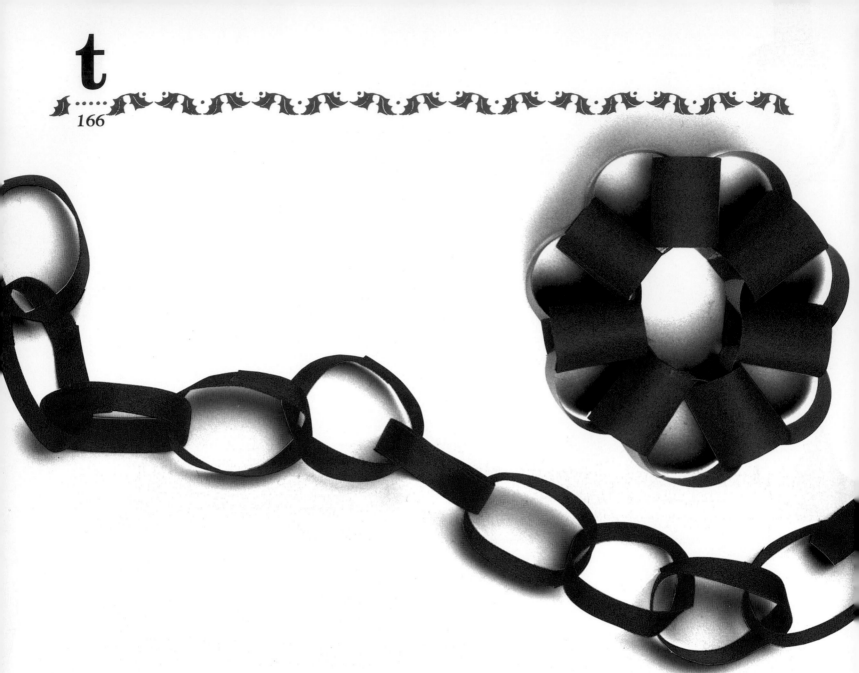

ORNAMENTAL "PAPER" CHAINS FOR THE CHRISTMAS TREE

Children have been making paper chains for the Christmas tree as long as there have been Christmas trees and construction paper. Most of us have experienced the dismay of taking out a box of tree decorations and lifting out fathom upon fathom of faded and crushed paper chain from years past. What do you do with such a sad relic? Should it be ceremonially burned like an old flag? Or do you unceremoniously sneak it into the trash when no one's looking?

There is no help for the old construction paper chain: it must go out. But there are fresh and distinctive looks to be created with *new* versions of paper chains. Some will even with-

stand the ravages of weeks on the Christmas tree and a year in storage.

Children can make chains of strips cut from colorful advertisements, or sliced-up, discarded drawings from school interspersed with brightly colored stationery. Some stores have a brand of paper called Paper-by-the-Pound. Although the sheets are smaller than construction paper, the colors are brighter and more durable, and the paper itself is easier to manipulate. The cost is comparable, and you only buy the colors you like.

Grown-ups and older children can make fine, long chains with finer pieces of paper, only a quarter-inch wide, either cutting it from the above-mentioned stationery or buying it as wide quilling paper. Wide, shiny curling ribbon is another striking and easy-to-obtain paper chain material. Buy it

in soft colors or bright Mylar, depending on the mood of your Christmas tree. "Real" satin ribbon, the woven kind with selvedges on the sides, has both richness and an old-fashioned look. For an exciting, up-town chain, try using glossy curl ribbon in bright fire colors—purples, reds, oranges, deep yellow.

Materials:

strips of ribbon, wide quilling paper, or brightly colored paper (the width of the strips depends on how wide you want your chains to be)

scissors or paper cutter

rubber cement or white craft glue (Most ribbon does not stick well with white glue. Rubber cement works well, but be sure your work area is well ventilated if you use it.)

Individual paper chains:

1. Using scissors or a paper cutter, cut one or more strips of colored paper or ribbon. The dimensions are unimportant as long as the strip is at least four times as long as it is wide. Make all the links of one chain roughly the same size.

2. Glue the ends of one strip together to form a circle. Pass a new strip through the circle and glue the ends together to form another circle attached to the first. Continue adding links until the chain is as long as you want it.

3. Have an adult drape the chain on the Christmas tree, over a doorway, or along the banister, or anywhere else that looks nice.

◆ **Mass produced chains:**
(In addition to the materials above, you will need clear tape.)

Here is a system for adults or older children for mass producing chains. Most young children occupy themselves happily cutting and gluing individual strips.

1. Cut many pieces of ribbon or strips of paper to desired length (at least four times the width). Arrange them for gluing side by side along a length of tape.

2. Smear rubber cement on tips of one side; turn the whole tape over and smear rubber cement on the *other* side of the other end of the ribbons. Hang the tape from the edge of your work table. Let the glue dry. (When rubber cement dries, it functions as contact cement.)

◆ 3. Prepare a similar tape for each color. Hang tapes separately on the edge of your work table.

4. Take strips one by one and form them into circles, linking each one to the one before, and pressing the links closed with your thumb and index finger.

Suggestion: A paper chain of 14 fat links 2 by ¾ inches can be formed into a rosette by linking the 14th link to the first.

Trees trimmed with homemade ornaments are trees trimmed with memories. Other personalized decoration ideas: felt and wooden cutouts of snowmen, doves, hearts, horses, and angels, shining with sequins; chocolate-chip cookies strung on ribbons; whole nutmegs and cinnamon sticks; and nosegays of rosemary.

Twelve Days of Christmas

In America and other northern countries, Christmas means a day of celebration—with Christmas Eve, two days at the most. The workers return to their jobs until the New Year's Eve festivities commence.

But traditionally, the Christmas celebration spanned twelve days and ended with Epiphany, or Twelfth Night, on January 6. The shortening of the twelve days is thought to be due to the Industrial Revolution, which limited the number of vacation days allowed to workers. The typically long midwinter festivals of history may also have been sabotaged over the years by the increased popularity of summer vacation. In any case, the old poem and carol "The Twelve Days of Christmas," signifies the historic importance of this jovial period. (*See also Christmas; December 25; Epiphany.*)

THE TWELVE DAYS OF CHRISTMAS

On the first day of Christmas my true love sent to me
A partridge in a pear tree.
On the second day of Christmas my true love sent to me
Two turtle doves and a partridge in a pear tree.
On the third day of Christmas my true love sent to me
Three french hens, etc…
On the fourth day of Christmas my true love sent to me
Four calling birds, etc…
On the fifth day of Christmas my true love sent to me
Five golden rings, etc…
On the sixth day of Christmas my true love sent to me
Six geese a-laying, etc…
On the seventh day of Christmas my true love sent to me
Seven swans a-swimming, etc…
On the eighth day of Christmas my true love sent to me
Eight maids a-milking, etc…
On the ninth day of Christmas my true love sent to me
Nine pipers piping, etc…
On the tenth day of Christmas my true love sent to me
Ten drummers drumming, etc…
On the eleventh day of Christmas my true love sent to me
Eleven lords a-leaping, etc…
On the twelfth day of Christmas my true love sent to me
Twelve ladies dancing, etc…

V

"A Visit From St. Nicholas"

When Clement Clarke Moore wrote a poem about a man "dressed all in furs" for his children in 1822, little did he know that his fictional Christmas Eve would shape the image of many such nights to come. The Dutch are credited with bringing the story of St. Nicholas himself to America (many European countries still celebrate the Feast of St. Nicholas on December 6), but it was Moore who popularized the notion that St. Nicholas drove his eight flying reindeer and a sleigh over the rooftops and slid down the chimney on Christmas Eve.

"A Visit From St. Nicholas" was first published in 1823 in the Troy, New York, *Sentinel*—a visitor to Moore's home originally heard him read the poem to his six children and received permission to publish it a year later. However, Moore did not acknowledge that he was the author until 1837, since he was most proud of his work as a professor in a New York Theological seminary and his authorship of a Hebrew dictionary. Moore died in 1863 at the age of 84, but his poem continues to delight children more than a century later. *(See also Santa Claus; Poems and Stories.)*

A VISIT FROM ST. NICHOLAS

Clement C. Moore

'Twas the night before Christmas, when all
   through the house
Not a creature was stirring, not even a mouse;
The stockings were hung by the chimney with care,
In hopes that St. Nicholas soon would be there;
The children were nestled all snug in their beds,
While visions of sugar-plums danced in their heads;
And Mamma in her kerchief, and I in my cap,
Had just settled our brains for a long winter's nap,
When out on the lawn there arose such a clatter,
I sprang from the bed to see what was the matter.
Away to the window I flew like a flash,
Tore open the shutters and threw up the sash.
The moon on the breast of the new-fallen snow
Gave the lustre of midday to objects below,
When, what to my wondering eyes should appear,
But a miniature sleigh, and eight tiny reindeer,
With a little old driver, so lively and quick,
I knew in a moment it must be St. Nick.
More rapid than eagles his coursers they came,
And he whistled, and shouted, and called them
   by name:
"Now, Dasher! now Dancer! now Prancer
   and Vixen!
On, Comet! on, Cupid! on, Donner and Blitzen!
To the top of the porch! to the top of the wall!
Now dash away! dash away! dash away all!"
As dry leaves that before the wild hurricane fly,
When they meet with an obstacle, mount to the sky,
So up to the house-top the coursers they flew,

With the sleigh full of toys, and St. Nicholas too.
And then, in a twinkling, I heard on the roof
The prancing and pawing of each little hoof.
As I drew in my head, and was turning around,
Down the chimney St. Nicholas came with a bound.
He was dressed all in fur, from his head to his foot,
And his clothes were all tarnished with ashes
   and soot;
A bundle of toys he had flung on his back,
And he looked like a pedlar just opening his pack.
His eyes—how they twinkled! his dimples how merry!
His cheeks were like roses, his nose like a cherry!
His droll little mouth was drawn up like a bow,
And the beard of his chin was as white as the snow;
The stump of a pipe he held tight in his teeth,
And the smoke it encircled his head like a wreath;
He had a broad face and a little round belly,
That shook when he laughed, like a bowlful of jelly.
He was chubby and plump, a right jolly old elf,
And I laughed when I saw him, in spite of myself;
A wink of his eye and a twist of his head
Soon gave me to know I had nothing to dread.
He spoke not a word, but went straight to his work,
And filled all the stockings; then turned with a jerk,
And laying his finger aside of his nose,
And giving a nod, up the chimney he rose;
He sprang to his sleigh, to his team gave a whistle,
And away they all flew like the down of a thistle.
But I heard him exclaim, ere he drove out of sight,
"Happy Christmas to all and to all a good night!"

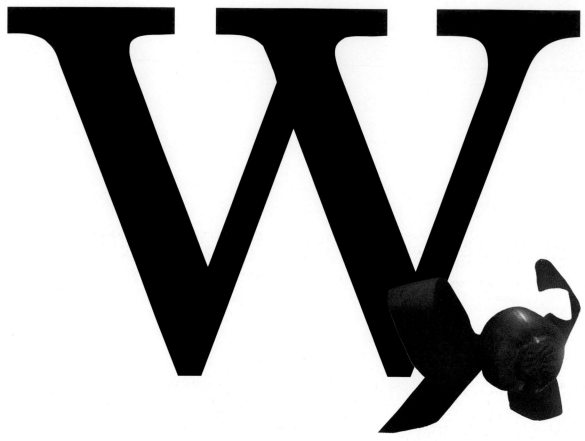

WASSAIL BOWL

Here is a wonderful recipe for the traditional English Christmas punch, wassail.

5 pints beer
2 cups sherry
2½ cups brown sugar, packed
1 lemon, sliced
1 teaspoon ginger
3 slices white bread, crusts removed,
   cut into star shapes and toasted

In a large saucepan, gently heat the beer with the sherry. Add the remaining ingredients, stirring and cooking over low heat until blended. Float toast stars on the surface just before serving.
Makes 15 servings

White Christmas

Snow is the crowning touch to a perfect Christmas. Holiday cards, store windows, and even televised-Christmas-show sets sentimentalize the image of snow on treetops, mailboxes, and windowsills. Without this meteorologic phenomenon there would be no sleighs and snowmen—important symbols of the holiday season.

Manufacturers create plastic and spray-can facsimiles of snow to decorate our trees and windows. And many a Christmas story occurs amid a shower of lacy flakes.

Two Christmas storytellers are believed responsible for the myth that yesterday's Christmases were always snowy. When Charles Dickens wrote of Mr. Pickwick and Scrooge, he covered the rooftops with snow, the lakes with ice. In "A Visit From St. Nicholas," Clement C. Moore saw to it that Santa had snow for his sleigh.

Yet, records show that in England and North America alike, snow at Christmas is unusual. Californians and Southerners, for example, are more apt to celebrate the holidays in their shirt sleeves. Even New Englanders can recall a recent Christmas with 50-degree-plus weather, in all probability more recent than a white Christmas. And although

"I have often thought, says Sir Roger, it happens very well that Christmas should fall in the middle of winter."
—Joseph Addison, The Spectator (1712)

records show that snow truly did fall on many Christmases in Dickens's childhood, during the rest of his lifetime—and in most of Moore's—grey Christmases were more common.

So in actuality, Christmases have never been particularly snowy, although Irving Berlin might have disagreed. He wrote the song "White Christmas" for the 1940 film *Holiday Inn*, and it is second only to "Silent Night" as the best-loved and most frequently heard song about the holiday. Starring Bing Crosby and Fred Astaire, *Holiday Inn*'s plot concerns a romantic triangle and the establishment of a country inn that's only open on holidays. Berlin wrote other holiday songs for the film, but when Bing Crosby sang "White Christmas" he helped it win an Oscar.

During World War II, "White Christmas" became a favorite of the soldiers, reminding them nostalgically of home and the holiday season. The song maintained its popularity after the war as well: Bing Crosby's recording alone sold about 25 million records. In a quarter of a century the song sold about four million copies of sheet music in 115 different arrangements, and was recorded over three hundred times, with sales totaling around 50 million records.

In 1954 "White Christmas" inspired another musical film of the same title. Also an Irving Berlin production, the movie starred Rosemary Clooney, Bing Crosby, Vera-Ellen, and Danny Kaye and partially reworked *Holiday Inn* with a plot about army buddies Crosby and Kaye boosting the popularity of a winter resort run by their ex-officer. Although the film was not met with as much critical acclaim as *Holiday Inn*, it became Berlin's greatest money-maker and is still played on the networks every year. (*See also Dickens, Charles; Moore, Clement C.; Movies; Music.*)

Wise Men

According to the story of the first Christmas, three Wise Men sought the infant Jesus to worship and present him with gifts. The original story from the Bible's book of Matthew offers very few details:

Now when Jesus was born in Bethlehem of Judea in the days of Herod the king, behold, there came wise men from the east to Jerusalem, saying, Where is he that is born King of Jews? for we have seen his star in the east, and are come to worship him. (St. Matthew 2:1-2)

And when they were come into the house, they saw the young child with Mary his mother, and fell down, and worshipped him: and when they had opened their treasures, they presented unto him gifts; gold, and frankincense, and myrrh. (St. Matthew 2:11)

Yet legend and the opinion of historians tells us more about these mysterious visitors. The trio is thought to represent three stages of life. Melchior, King of Arabia, was supposedly sixty years old and had a long beard and a small frame. Balthasar, King of Ethiopia, was reputedly a bearded, black man of forty. And Caspar (also known as Gaspar or Kaspar), King of

"Dashing through the snow in a one-horse open sleigh; O'er the fields we go, laughing all the way."
—John Pierpont, Jingle Bells (1856)

Taursus, was twenty, tall, and beardless.

The three kings are said to have watched the sky patiently waiting for the realization of the Jewish prophecy that a bright star would announce salvation. When the star did actually appear, it led them to Jerusalem, where they met with King Herod (as told in Matthew 2:7-8). Herod had learned from the prophets that Christ would be born in Bethlehem, and pretending to welcome the child's arrival, told the wise men to find him "and bring me word."

The visitors did, indeed, find Jesus, and after they had rejoiced and presented their gifts, legend has it that Mary gave them the white linen bands

According to the Bible narrative of the Nativity, the visitors from the East were not kings but Magi (priests of the ancient Medes and Persians), and the number was not restricted to three. Historians have supplied many of the details that we know as the story of the first Christmas.

that once clothed the baby. But instead of returning to Herod, the Bible says the wise men were warned by God in a dream to take another route to return

to their countries (Matthew 2:12). According to tradition, the wise men subsequently gave up their kingdoms, distributed their properties to the poor, and went out to preach the gospel.

Some authorities assert that the visit of the Wise Men occurred on January 6, the day on which Twelfth Night, or Epiphany, is designated by the church. The Wise Men are not only an essential part of nativity scenes, they figure prominently in Christmas carols and in works of art. Other than the three kings, the Wise Men are also known as the "Magi," which was a sect of priests among the ancient Medes and Persians known for their great wisdom. (*See also Epiphany; The First Christmas; Frankincense; Gold.*)

Wreath

The most popular of all door decorations, the wreath has become a gesture of holiday welcome. The outdoor wreath is a recent innovation, but circles of fresh evergreens have been used to decorate homes since Victorian times.

Wreaths can be bought or handmade, and there are a great many styles. The Advent wreath is a circle of fir decorated with four candles, each of which ✦ is lit on one of the four Sundays before Christmas. Wreaths may be made entirely of pinecones, as is the Scandinavian and Italian custom, or fashioned from dried flowers and herbs the way they were made in England during the Middle Ages. A simple wreath may be made of mixed greens, and decorated with cones, bayberry, and red berries; more elaborate types might be decorated with shellacked fruits. (*See also Advent; Evergreens; International* ✦ *Christmases.*)

✦ *Xmas*

In Greek, X is the first letter of Christ's name (ch). Therefore, X was taken to represent the word "Christ" in the early Christian Church. Xmas is still used today, but ironically, some modern-day Christians object to writing the holiday's name in this fashion. The belief is that using Xmas instead of Christmas further contributes to the commercialism of the holiday, that it "takes the Christ out of Christmas." *(See also Commercialism.)*

"Let us kneel with Mary Maid, With Joseph bent and hoary, With saint and angel, ox and ass, To hail the King of Glory."
—Christina Rossetti (1830-1894), Let Us Kneel with Mary Maid

X
.....
179

Y

♦ Yes, Virginia (There is a Santa Claus)

On September 21, 1897, a letter from an eight-year-old girl, Virginia O'Hanlon, appeared in *The New York Sun,* beseeching the editors to answer her question, "Is there a Santa Claus?"

"Yes, Virginia, there is a Santa Claus," was the reply by Francis Pharcellus Church, who is credited for the most famous editorial response in history. The *Sun* reran Church's editorial to introduce the Christmas season each year until the newspaper's demise more than half a century later. Church died in New York City on April 11, 1906; Virginia O'Hanlon Douglas died in 1971 at the age of eighty-two. Yet their heartfelt words will live on forever. ♦

Dear Editor

I am eight years old. Some of my friends say there is no such thing as Santa Claus. Papa says "If you see it in the Sun it's so." Please tell me the truth, is there a Santa Claus?

Virginia O'Hanlon
115 West Ninety-Fifth Street

Virginia, your little friends are wrong. They have been affected by the skepticism of a skeptical age. They do not believe except (what) they see. They think that nothing can be which is not comprehensible by their little minds. All minds, Virginia, whether they be men's or children's, are little. In this great universe of ours man is a mere insect, an ant, in his intellect, as compared with the boundless world about him, as measured by the intelligence capable of grasping the whole truth and knowledge.

Yes, Virginia, there is a Santa Claus. He exists as certainly as love and generosity and devotion exist, and you know that they abound and give to your life its highest beauty and joy. Alas! how dreary would be the world if there were no Santa Claus! It would be as dreary as if there were no Virginias. There would be no child-like faith then, no poetry, no romance to make tolerable this existence. We should have no enjoyment except in sense and sight. The eternal light with which childhood fills the world would be extinguished.

Not believe in Santa Claus! You might as well not believe in fairies! You might get your papa to hire men to watch in all the chimneys on Christmas Eve to catch Santa Claus, but even if they did not see Santa Claus coming down, what would that prove? Nobody sees Santa Claus, but that is no sign that there is no Santa Claus. The most real things in the world are those that neither children nor men can see. Did you ever see fairies dancing on the lawn? Of course not, but that's no proof that they are not there. Nobody can conceive or imagine all the wonders there are unseen and unseeable in the world.

You tear apart the baby's rattle and see what makes the noise inside, but there is a veil covering the unseen world which not the strongest man, nor even the united strength of all the strongest men that ever lived, could tear apart. Only faith, fancy, poetry, love, romance, can push aside that curtain and view and picture the supernal beauty and glory beyond. Is it all real? Ah, Virginia, in all this world there is nothing else real and abiding.

No Santa Claus! Thank God! he lives, and he lives forever. A thousand years from now, Virginia, nay, times ten thousand years from now, he will continue to make glad the heart of childhood.

Yule Log

The custom of burning a Yule log comes from the Norse and Anglo-Saxons, who burned a huge oak log once a year to honor Thor, the god of Thunder. When the northern tribes accepted Christianity, their old winter celebration was replaced by Christmas, or Juul, as it was known in Northern Europe. Selecting and burning the Yule log then became symbolic of Christ as Light of the World, and many different nationalities came to accept this custom as their own with variations in their rituals.

In England, for example, many people selected oak, pine, or ash logs; the Scottish people preferred those from birches; and Yugoslavians usually chose oak alone. In France, often the entire family dressed in their best clothes and went out to the woods together. In Norway the father went out alone to bring in the log.

But in most cases, going for "the Christmas brand"—the largest that one's fireplace would accommodate—was cause for a big celebration. Once the tree was cut and the designated section of the trunk secured, the log might be draped with garlands and escorted home with a parade. Songs were sung and horns were blown as the procession moved along. After dragging the log into the home, the merrymakers might pray over, drink to, sit on, or kiss the log for luck. In Italy, the entire family gathered around the guest of honor and the boys and girls struck it hard with sticks. Eventually, the log was lit with an unburned part of the previous year's log—particularly in England, where the marriage of the old and new was considered to bring good luck.

Several other superstitions developed around the Yule log as well. After the traditional games that took place in front of the burning log were played out (diving for apples in a tub of cold water, sack races, tying hands behind one's back and trying to eat Yule cakes that hung from the rafters), the log was allowed to burn through the night. But it was considered bad luck for the entire year if the fire failed to last. In some Slavic lands, the household members would not disturb the embers for fear that their ancestors would fall into hell. The ashes of the Yule log were often buried at the roots of fruit trees to make them more fruitful. In some countries, ashes were saved to cure tooth-aches and to rid cats of pests.

Today the Yule log tradition is still carried out in the countries that fostered it. Since America's ancestry is rich with northern Europeans, the Yule log has been an important part of Christmas in this country as well. For example, in the Old South it was customary to give the slaves a vacation for as long as the Christmas log burned. Stories have it that the slaves sprinkled the log with water to keep the fire going, so any water-logged tree was, in consequence, known as "having as much water as a Christmas log." (*See also International Christmases.*)

At an early stage in the history of the Yule log the spirits of the departed were believed to be present in the glowing embers of the hearth. According to European tradition, shoes and stockings were put near the fireplace for the same reason an old boot was associated with a wedding: to bring good luck and drive away evil spirits.

Kitchen Metrics

For cooking and baking convenience, the Metric Commission of Canada suggests the following for adapting to metric measurement. The table gives approximate, rather than exact, conversions.

SPOONS

1/4 teaspoon = 1 milliliter

1/2 teaspoon = 2 milliliters

1 teaspoon = 5 milliliters

1 tablespoon = 15 milliliters

2 tablespoons = 25 milliliters

3 tablespoons = 50 milliliters

CUPS

1/4 cup = 50 milliliters

1/3 cup = 75 milliliters

1/2 cup = 125 milliliters

2/3 cup = 150 milliliters

3/4 cup = 175 milliliters

1 cup = 250 milliliters

OVEN TEMPERATURES

200°F = 100°C	350°F = 180°C
225°F = 110°C	375°F = 190°C
250°F = 120°C	400°F = 200°C
275°F = 140°C	425°F = 220°C
300°F = 150°C	450°F = 230°C
325°F = 160°C	475°F = 240°C

TO ADAPT MASS

one ounce = 28 grams

one pound = .45 kilograms

TO ADAPT LENGTH

one inch = 2.5 centimeters

one foot = 30 centimeters

one yard = .9 meters

Bibliography

Charlton, Jim. *A Christmas Companion. Recipes, Traditions and and Customs from Around the World.* New York: Perigee Books, 1989.

Chrisman, Irma. *Christmas Trees, Decorations and Ornaments.* New York: Hearthside Press, 1956.

Crager, Meg. *The Whole Christmas Catalogue.* Tucson, Arizona: HP Books, 1986.

December 25th: The Joys of Christmas Past. New York: Dodd, Mead & Company, 1955.

Dickens, Charles. *The Annotated Christmas Carol.* New York: Potter, 1976.

Ewen, David. *Great Men of American Popular Song.* Englewood Cliffs, NJ: Prentice-Hall, 1970.

Faith, William Robert. *Bob Hope: A Life in Comedy.* New York: G.P. Putnam's Sons, 1982.

Farm Journal Christmas Idea Book. Philadelphia: Countryside Press, 1970.

Foley, Daniel J. *Christmas in the Good Old Days.* Philadelphia: Chilton Company, 1961.

Hartman, Tom, ed. *Guinness Book of Christmas.* London: Guinness Books, 1984.

Hemingway, Beth. *A Second Treasury of Christmas Decorations.* New York: Hearthside Press, 1961.

Kainen, Ruth Cole. *America's Christmas Heritage.* New York: Funk and Wagnalls, 1969.

Krythe, Maymie R. *All About Christmas.* New York: Harper & Brothers, 1954.

Lawhead, Alice Slaikeu. *The Christmas Book. Westchester, Illinois:* Crossway Books, 1985.

Moore, Clement C. *The Night Before Christmas: A Visit From St. Nicholas.* New York: Dover Publications, 1971.

Newcombe, Jack, ed. *A Christmas Treasury.* New York: The Viking Press, 1982.

Parents Magazine's Christmas Holiday Book. New York: Parents Magazine Press, 1972.

Posselt, Eric, ed. *The World's Greatest Christmas Stories.* New York: Prentice Hall, 1950.

Pox, Noel. *Simply Christmas: How to Have a Non-Commercial Christmas.* New York: Walker and Company, 1980.

Robinson, Jo, and Jean Coppock Staeheli. *Unplug the Christmas Machine: How to Have the Christmas You've Always Wanted.* New York: William Morrow and Co., 1982.

Sansom, William. *A Book of Christmas.* New York: McGraw, 1968.

The Saturday Evening Post Christmas Book. Indianapolis: Curtis Publishing, 1976.

Schott, Webster, ed. *American Christmas.* Kansas City: Hallmark, 1967.

Schuler, Stanley. *Outdoor Lighting For Your Home.* Princeton: Van Nostrand, 1962.

Slaikeu Lawhead, Alice. *The Christmas Book.* Westchester, IL: Crossway Books, 1985.

Snyder, Phillip. *The Christmas Tree Book.*

Stewart, Linda Martin, ed., *Christmas is Coming!* Birmingham, Alabama: Oxmoor House, 1987.

The Time-Life Book of Christmas. New York: Prentice Hall Press, 1987.

The Time-Life Book of Christmas. Englewood Cliffs, NJ: Prentice Hall, 1987.

Tucker, Kristin M., and Rebecca Lowe Warren. *Celebrate the Wonder: A Family Christmas Treasury.* New York: Ballantine, 1988.

Van Dyke, Henry. *"Even unto Bethlehem:" The Story of Christmas.* New York: Scribner, 1928.

Voce, Jo, and Candace N. Conard, eds. *The Joy of Christmas.* Birmingham, Alabama: Oxmoor House, 1982.

Wagenknecht, Edward. *The Fireside Book of Christmas Stories.* Indianapolis: Bobbs, 1945.

Wertsner, Anne. *Make Your Own Merry Christmas.* New York: Stratford Press, 1950.

Index

PHOTO CREDITS